Cambridge Elements ≡

Elements in International Relations
edited by
Jon C. W. Pevehouse
University of Wisconsin–Madison
Tanja A. Börzel
Freie Universität Berlin
Edward D. Mansfield
University of Pennsylvania
Associate Editors – International Relations Theory
Jeffrey T. Checkel, European
University Institute, Florence

LOCKEAN LIBERALISM IN INTERNATIONAL RELATIONS

Alexandru V. Grigorescu
Loyola University Chicago
Claudio J. Katz
Loyola University Chicago

CAMBRIDGE
UNIVERSITY PRESS

CAMBRIDGE
UNIVERSITY PRESS

Shaftesbury Road, Cambridge CB2 8EA, United Kingdom

One Liberty Plaza, 20th Floor, New York, NY 10006, USA

477 Williamstown Road, Port Melbourne, VIC 3207, Australia

314–321, 3rd Floor, Plot 3, Splendor Forum, Jasola District Centre,
New Delhi – 110025, India

103 Penang Road, #05–06/07, Visioncrest Commercial, Singapore 238467

Cambridge University Press is part of Cambridge University Press & Assessment,
a department of the University of Cambridge.

We share the University's mission to contribute to society through the pursuit of
education, learning and research at the highest international levels of excellence.

www.cambridge.org
Information on this title: www.cambridge.org/9781009517003

DOI: 10.1017/9781009516952

When citing this work, please include a reference to the DOI 10.1017/9781009516952

First published 2024

A catalogue record for this publication is available from the British Library.

ISBN 978-1-009-51700-3 Hardback
ISBN 978-1-009-51698-3 Paperback
ISSN 2515-706X (online)
ISSN 2515-7302 (print)

Lockean Liberalism in International Relations

Elements in International Relations

DOI: 10.1017/9781009516952
First published online: March 2024

Alexandru V. Grigorescu
Loyola University Chicago

Claudio J. Katz
Loyola University Chicago

Author for correspondence: Alexandru V. Grigorescu, agrigor@luc.edu

Abstract: This Element applies a new version of liberalism to international relations (IR), one that derives from the political theory of John Locke. It begins with a survey of liberal IR theories, showing that the main variants of this approach have all glossed over classical liberalism's core concern: fear of the state's concentrated power and the imperative of establishing institutions to restrain its inevitable abuse. The authors tease out from Locke's work its "realist" elements: his emphasis on politics, power, and restraints on power (the "Lockean tripod"). They then show how this Lockean approach (1) complements existing liberal approaches and answers some of the existing critiques directed toward them, (2) offers a broader analytical framework for several very different strands of IR literature, and (3) has broad theoretical and practical implications for international relations.

Keywords: IR theory, liberalism, Locke, international organizations, restraints on power

ISBNs: 9781009517003 (HB), 9781009516983 (PB), 9781009516952 (OC)
ISSNs: 2515-706X (online), 2515-7302 (print)

Contents

1 The Evolution of Liberal Thought in IR and the Missing "Lockean" Original Variant

Introduction

Theories focusing on politics *within* the state and those in international relations (IR), studying politics *among* states, have tended to follow different evolutionary paths. At times, the two appeared to have little in common. For instance, in the first few decades after World War II, theorists such as Charles Manning, Frederick Dunn, and Stanley Hoffman advocated establishing IR as a separate field from political science. In 1959, Hoffman wrote: "International Relations take place in a milieu which has its own 'coherence and uniqueness', its rules of the game which differ sharply from the rules of domestic politics, its own perspective" (Hoffmann, 1959: 347). Other times, IR scholars have sought to explain developments by drawing upon analogies to phenomena unfolding within states. Many analogies, however, were rejected as simplistic and flawed and, in fact, for a long time, led to a stigma against domestic-international parallels (Suganami, 2008).

And yet, this stigma has not diminished IR scholars' intermittent interest in domestic theoretical approaches at the broadest level, such as social constructivism, Marxism, or feminism, or even at the mezzo level, such as principal–agent theory, constitutionalism, or bureaucratic politics. As arguments have moved from the specific to the general, IR scholarship has been more likely to accept domestic parallels.

Liberalism is perhaps the broadest and most widely cited theoretical tradition derived from domestic politics and applied to IR. Liberal political theory, developed over almost half a millennium, has assumed different forms as political theorists reinterpreted it to address new circumstances and concerns. International relations theory, generally considered to have only truly emerged after World War I, has frequently borrowed from diverse variants of liberalism as applied to domestic politics. This process has led to different forms of liberalism in IR labeled (correctly or not) "idealism,"[1] "liberal internationalism," "neoliberal institutionalism," or "new liberalism."[2]

In this first section, we show that, while all of these approaches are fruitful in explaining international developments and as starting points for normative

---

[1] As we will show, recent literature identifies multiple forms of IR liberalism in the approaches that are often subsumed under the broader interwar idealist label. These strands of liberalism share some common traits but also exhibit certain differences with each other, as well as with other forms of IR liberalism that emerged in the late twentieth century. See, e.g., Long and Wilson (2003).

[2] For comprehensive discussions of these four forms of IR liberalism as well as other IR theoretical approaches see, e.g., Reus-Smit and Snidal (2008).

arguments about how best to organize international politics, they all miss (or gloss over) the core concern of classical liberalism: fear of concentrated power and the purposeful establishment of institutions to restrain its abuse. Classical liberalism emerged in great part as a reaction to the increasing power of sovereigns in the sixteenth and seventeenth centuries and to the writings of theorists who justified unconditional obedience to absolute monarchy, either on religious grounds, such as Jacques-Bénigne Bossuet and Robert Filmer, or secular ones, such as Jean Bodin and Thomas Hobbes. We argue that analogous dynamics leading to power concentration in individual states and in international institutions, where dominant states often impose their will on smaller states by pooling their aggregate power, require that we pay greater attention to mechanisms that restrain such power. As in the domestic realm, where the concentration of power in the hands of individual governments has both increased and decreased, the international realm has gone through periods when individual states have amassed formidable amounts of relative power (as Britain in the late nineteenth century or the United States immediately after World War II) and others where power was dispersed across multiple dominant states (as during the interwar era or over the past decade or two). Similarly, international institutions came to be extraordinarily influential at times of greater cooperation between powerful states, as in the early nineteenth century when the Concert of Europe imposed the will of the five great European powers, or the 1990s and early 2000s when intergovernmental organizations (IGOs) such as the IMF, World Bank, EU, and even the UN Security Council (themselves also backed by powerful states), wielded extraordinary power over weak states, influencing their policies in ways that had not been possible just a few decades earlier. While the IR literature has touched upon the need for restraints on powerful states and, to some degree, even on powerful international institutions, we will show that it can benefit from a broad approach that draws from classical liberalism.

Most important, we posit that, despite his essential role in founding the liberal tradition, IR scholars have scarcely used Locke's political theory to inform their analyses or normative concerns. In the next section, we balance existing normative interpretations of Locke with an additional one stressing his "realist" approach. We also complement his main arguments with those of several subsequent classical liberals. We highlight three essential elements of the Lockean and, more broadly, the classical liberal approach – politics, power, and restraints on power – and derive three corresponding principles that need to be balanced as part of a delicate "tripod."[3] The third section of this study

---

[3] We use this term in part to draw a parallel with the "Kantian tripod" that the IR literature has discussed at length (e.g., Russett et al., 1998).

explains how a Lockean version of liberalism applies to the international realm and offers a perspective that enhances our understanding of IR.

Before concluding this section laying out the plan of our Element, it is important to explain the reasons that led us to select Locke's political theory as a starting point for our analysis. First, Locke was a champion of limited government: his liberalism is a political theory of institutionalized "fences," driven by the fear of the state's arbitrary exercise of power, an essential argument that has long been applied to domestic systems but has not yet been applied to the international realm.[4] We argue that by focusing on Locke and classical liberalism, we recover the missing and necessary third "leg" of the tripod, emphasizing power restraints. This allows us to balance not just existing forms of IR liberalism, but also the dominant IR realist approach that has (over) emphasized power.

Locke indeed launched the liberal tradition, giving it its original persuasive force (Zuckert, 2002). Classical liberalism's lineages were deeply influenced by him, and interpretations of Locke's thought have standardly served as ways of reinterpreting liberalism's various strands (Bell, 2014; Tully, 1993). By the late eighteenth century, classical liberals such as Montesquieu, Kant, and the authors of *The Federalist* subscribed to Locke's view that the constitutional dispersion of power and the rule of law formed essential safeguards against the danger of despotism. These theorists of course made their own unique contributions to classical liberalism, drawing on distinct intellectual traditions to address specific historical challenges. Nevertheless, we shall expand our field of vision from Locke to these classical liberals because, and to the extent that, they share and complement a recognizably Lockean fear of concentrated power and an overriding concern to limit its arbitrary exercise.

Classical liberalism's very success, however, paradoxically meant that liberal theorists have tended to shift their focus away from its original concerns. Indeed, Shklar (1989: 21) writes that "in the course of so many years of ideological conflict [liberalism] seems to have lost its identity completely. Overuse and overextension have rendered it so amorphous that it can now serve as an all-purpose word, whether of abuse or praise" (see also Bell, 2014). Mill (1989 [1859]: 5–9), in his own reconstruction of liberalism's evolution, maintained that liberal theorists reconsidered their defenses of personal liberty as the public progressively succeeded in limiting "the power which the ruler should be suffered to exercise over the community," from "the establishment of constitutional checks" on the ruler's power, to a "new demand for

---

[4] Locke repeatedly employs "fences" as a metaphor to underscore the need to restrain the power of the state (Locke, 1967 [1690]: sect. 17, 93, 136, 222). This text, as well as the "First Treatise," will be henceforth cited in the text by section number(s).

elective and temporary rulers," to a fear of "'the tyranny of the majority',"
which "is now generally included among the evils against which society
requires to be on its guard." By the nineteenth and twentieth centuries, institutional restraints on state power such as independent courts and parliamentary
assemblies spread across states, and were therefore less likely to be problem-
atized by liberal theorists.[5] This shift is perhaps most evident in the work of
John Rawls, the most dominant figure in contemporary liberal political thought,
who emphasized the importance of establishing fair terms of social cooperation
over institutional constraints on the power of the state (Rawls, 2001: 7–8).

A second advantage of turning to Locke's work, in addition to his focus on the
need to restrain the state's power, is his "realism,"[6] which complements existing
forms of IR liberalism in ways that allow it to find some common ground with
the realist IR approach. This is not to ignore Locke's normative commitments.
Rather, our claim is that the literature on Locke has exaggerated his political
moralism at the expense of his emphasis on the dynamics of power. Here, too,
we shall draw on the writings of classical liberals because and to the extent that
they share Locke's realist approach – a concern with politics as the alternative to
violence, a focus on the effective concentration of state power as the solution to
domestic anarchy, and the paramount need to develop institutional mechanisms
to restrain its abuse.[7]

The following six subsections summarize the main arguments of the various
strands of existing IR liberalism as well as of other theoretical approaches that could
have led to a response building on Lockean liberalism. We show that virtually all
such theories neglected or downplayed one or more elements of the Lockean tripod.
While the literature has pointed out the problems that derive from the lack of
emphasis on politics and/or power in some existing liberal IR approaches, it has

---

[5] Tocqueville and Mill turned their attention to the problem of protecting liberty from the danger of
a growing mass culture. US Progressives such as John Dewey and English New Liberals such as
L. T. Hobhouse responded to the increasing social costs of a maturing capitalism, especially the
growing threat to liberty posed by the periodic dislocations and deepening class inequalities of the
turn of the century. These liberal theorists were also concerned to enlist the public power of the
state to restrain the private power of capitalist interests (see Kloppenberg, 1986).

[6] Although we find similar elements in realism in international relations and liberal realism in
political theory, these two bodies of literature are separate and have not truly acknowledged each
other. See, e.g., Sleat (2011: 469, n. 1).

[7] Classical liberals subscribed to constitutional guardrails to fence power and channel conflict
because they shared Locke's pessimism about the human capacity for moral restraint. As Kant
acknowledged (1970 [1795]: 112), "as hard as it may sound, the problem of setting up a state can
be solved even by a nation of devils." Madison's *Federalist* 51 (1961 [1788]: 349) famously
articulates the same problem: "But what is government itself but the greatest of all reflections on
human nature? If men were angels, no government would be necessary. If angels were to govern
men, neither external nor internal controuls on government would be necessary."

rarely addressed the absence of a direct focus on restraints on power, one of Locke's essential contributions to liberal political theory.

The Diverse Forms of IR Liberalism in the Interwar Era

Although political theorists had offered arguments related to relations among states for centuries, if not millennia, the systematic study of IR emerged as an independent field of inquiry after World War I. As this academic field was struggling to carve out its own identity, the urgency of adopting solutions to the problems that had led to the outbreak of the war prompted many scholars from established fields such as law, history, sociology, and economics, to offer a broad set of interpretations of the causes of the war and the policies needed to ensure a more peaceful world. Accordingly, the IR writings from that period frequently addressed narrow aspects of the broader theoretical approaches rather than overarching political theories and the connections between the various topics of trade, international organization, democracy, and peace to each other.

More specifically, scholars and practitioners writing in the aftermath of the war who are now labeled as "liberal" only rarely and vaguely linked their discussions of international politics to broader liberal traditions or to the writings of classical liberals. Any appeals to liberal political theorists made at the time were more likely to be to the economic liberalism of Smith, Ricardo and, most often, Cobden. Recent IR scholarship has explained in some detail the domestic-international connections in the debates that immediately followed World War I (e.g., Keohane, 1990; Long and Wilson, 2003; Richardson, 2001). It is primarily through these contemporary interpretations that we have come to identify the points of contact between the initial writings in IR theory and liberal political theory.

The IR liberalism of the early twentieth century was very diverse. Nevertheless, scholars distinguish three broad liberal perspectives that differed in the answers they offered to the question of which aspects of international relations, if any, needed to be regulated to foster peaceful coexistence. The first approach, termed "Cobdenite" (sometimes referred to as "old liberal internationalism") rejected economic and political regulation in the domestic and international realms, and may be best represented by the writings of Norman Angell (Long and Wilson, 2003: 314). This approach saw the war as a result of too much state intervention and therefore promoted a smaller role for governments in all realms. Although this view implied, of course, that state actions should be limited, it did not offer specific prescriptions regarding the use of institutions (domestic or international) to restrain power. In the aftermath of such a devastating war, many found this Cobdenite liberalism – a completely laissez-faire outlook in international politics and economics – difficult to accept as a general understanding that "something must be done" took hold. This first liberal perspective, therefore, was not very influential.

Two other international liberal approaches sought some form of intervention in international affairs and could be classified as part of a broader "regulatory liberalism" (Keohane, 1990). One of them, labeled "new" liberal internationalism, to distinguish it from the more traditional Cobdenite variant, saw laissez-faire economics in its pure form as at least partly responsible for the global economic contraction at the end of the nineteenth century. Thus, the defense of unregulated markets gave way to the need for social reform.

New liberal internationalist theorists did not, however, recommend strengthening the League of Nations, authorizing it to interfere in domestic *political* affairs. Rather, they promoted a more fluid set of organizations, focused on *economic* issues. David Mitrany, who later came to be known as the founder of functionalist IR theory, was perhaps the most important proponent of this group in academic circles (Long and Wilson, 2003). This emphasis on economic rather than political regulation implied that the approach sought more restraints on the domestic private sphere, not on governments.

The third group of liberals of that period was likely the largest and most vocal of the three discussed here. It consisted of individuals who were strong supporters of a powerful *political* role for international institutions, especially for the League of Nations. Interestingly, this group has been referred to, at least in some recent studies, as "Hobbesian liberals" (Long and Wilson, 2003). This term derived from the analogy commentators drew between Hobbes's prescription for a powerful government to end the English Civil War, a period of acute conflict that informed his conception of the "state of nature," and their prescription for powerful IGOs to contain conflict after World War I. The principle of collective security on which the League was established and the original intent authorizing it to intervene in interstate relations during war crises was considered by many scholars at that time to be in tune with the liberal emphasis on personal freedoms. Without such an international force, they argued, individuals would be left powerless in the face of another devastating world war. Proponents of this Hobbesian liberalism in IR include David Davies, James Shotwell, and Alfred Zimmern (Long and Wilson, 2003).

Those supporting the IR Hobbesian liberal approach, like other scholars of the interwar era, failed to make a connection to classical liberal fears of concentrated power and the need to restrain its abuse, although yet again such connections were not difficult to find. Indeed, a powerful League would be able to restrain *states*, especially the more powerful; but increasing the League's influence would also have the unintended consequence of allowing for even greater power concentration when the dominant states agreed on international policies. This Hobbesian "moment" in IR theory *could* readily have been followed by a classical liberal one. Such an approach, by analogy to Locke's critique of Hobbes, would have emphasized the potential dangers that power aggregation through international institutions like the League posed to the liberties of the many weak states and of the citizens of these states.[8] After all, the rules of the IGO had been shaped primarily by the most powerful states. During the negotiations that unfolded at its founding, small states had sought and used multiple arguments explaining why the new international rules needed to introduce mechanisms to restrain great powers from using these organizations as they pleased. But their representatives did not connect their arguments to liberal writings. Additionally, while those promoting small state influence in the League expressed apprehensions regarding the possible future actions of individual *states*, they did not appear to fear the massive collective power of all these dominant states or of the organization that now allowed for the aggregation of their power, in a similar way to the formation of the powerful Leviathan at the domestic level.[9]

One of the main reasons for this oversight may be that, after it became clear that the United States would not join the League and, later, when powerful states such as Germany, Italy, Japan, and the Soviet Union followed suit (and all hope of truly *collective* security failed), fears of a global Leviathan where the dominant states could come together to pool their considerable power, substantially subsided. Small states did not fear the League in the same way they came to fear IGOs (such as the World Bank, IMF, EU, or UNSC) toward the end of the twentieth century, as we discuss below. Moreover, multiple dominant states emerged from the war, not just one, as during the previous century or after World War II. In other words, the realities on the ground *at that time* did not encourage interwar liberalism to argue for further restraints on the concentrated power of and through international institutions in the same way that classical liberalism had promoted restraints on the powers of domestic governments. To paraphrase Locke, global governance in the aftermath of World War I did not produce a "lion," a concentration of power analogous to domestic governments,

---

[8] Another opportunity to connect the emerging League institutions and the notion of restraint on power came from the debates that took place *within* states (rather than among them), with regard to the power of the League. Perhaps most famously, Wilson's lost battle for US Senate ratification of the League Covenant touched upon important questions of sovereignty and, implicitly, of avoiding an all-powerful institution that would concentrate power, taking it away from individual states. This debate also did not lead to direct connections to classical liberal writings.

[9] Of course, similar Lockean arguments also could have been made regarding the Concert of Europe.

more threatening than the individual states that made up the international political system, analogous to the "polecats or foxes" Locke referred to in his description of the state of nature (2.93). Even the efforts to restrain the power of the most dominant states were not framed in this Lockean fashion.

In sum, the IR liberalism of the interwar era only drew on classical liberalism in an indirect fashion and, for the most part, in the economic realm, rather than the political one. Moreover, this early form of IR liberalism has been critiqued for its insufficient attention to two other important elements: the *politics* underlying states' interactions and the importance of *power disparities* between states in their interactions.

Indeed, interwar IR liberals stressed the existence of a "harmony of interests" among states, a concept that was at least partially inspired by Adam Smith's economic liberalism. They noted how the devastating aftermath of the Great War proved that all belligerents, in fact, had a shared interest in avoiding the global conflagration in the first place. They argued that states had failed to identify their common interests due primarily to poor communication and "secret covenants."[10] Accordingly, they promoted the need for open channels of communication between states. Their assumption was that, if secret diplomacy gave way to open communications in international relations, states would be able to identify their preexisting common goals, thus avoiding conflicts.

The focus on identifying areas of harmony downplayed any dissensus and eliminated the need for politics, understood as a continuous bargaining process in which actors with disparate interests come together to work out compromises among them. Early twentieth century liberalism in IR focused on how governments could uncover underlying, *already broadly accepted* solutions to the kinds of problems that had led to World War I, rather than on the process that allowed them to reach new solutions through the protracted give-and-take of political negotiations.

Carr and other realists who followed him rejected the notion that relations among states were harmonious. He noted that individuals' and the community's highest interests do not always coincide. At the international level, states had individual, often incompatible, *national* interests more often than *common* ones. It was, in fact, the interactions among states with different interests that constituted politics and that represented the true nature of IR. Carr (2001: 74) argued that the so-called harmonious interests are nothing more than the interests of the "dominant group which identifies itself with the community as a whole." This critique underscored the fact that IR liberals of the early twentieth century also

---

[10] Perhaps the best-known reference of the need to avoid secret diplomacy is the very first point of Wilson's Fourteen Point speech. See www.archives.gov/milestone-documents/president-woo drow-wilsons-14-points.

downplayed the importance of power relations. Indeed, the relatively egalitarian rules of the League did not give powerful states incentives to join or remain members of the IGO and, consequently, there was little power to back its decisions.

Hobbesian Arguments Adopted in IR after World War II

The outbreak of World War II, after numerous policies based on IR liberalism had been implemented specifically to avoid another major war, led to even more powerful attacks against this theoretical tradition, especially from the emergent realist approach. The connection between Hobbes's political theory and realism, in contrast to the liberal view of IR, was not as apparent as it now seems. First, as we saw, studies of interwar liberalism show that some authors drew parallels to Hobbes, at least in their support for strong IGOs and laws. Second, realism originally included important liberal elements. In fact, it did not emerge as a direct critique of liberalism but, rather, of idealism (or "utopianism," a word Carr used more often than, and interchangeably with, "idealism") (Long and Wilson, 2003: 4).

The best-known realist critics of idealism appeared to accept at least some liberal arguments. Carr (2001: 11), for instance, acknowledged that the "Cobdenite view of international trade" was a "real foundation" for international peace. Similarly, Morgenthau considered the role that international law can play in restraining power, yet another important liberal element (Morgenthau and Thompson, 1993).[11] In his landmark book, *Politics among Nations,* Morgenthau only mentioned Hobbes in passing, and in a way not related to our current interpretation of the theorist's influence on realism.

Kenneth Waltz, the "father" of neorealism, also did not draw directly from Hobbes. *Man, State, and War*, his first major work, focused on the flaws in Hobbes's work, considering it reductionist because it was based on individual level logics. He also questioned Hobbes's main contention that (strong) government brings about stability and peace. In an interesting "classical liberal" moment, Waltz (1979: 103) argued that "If the absence of government is associated with the threat of violence, so is its presence .... In the middle 1970s most inhabitants of Idi Amin's Uganda must have felt their lives becoming nasty, brutish, and short, quite as in Thomas Hobbes's state of nature."

---

[11] Morgenthau (in Morgenthau and Thompson 1993: 187) is actually the first to draw a parallel between the essential IR realist concept of balance of power and classical liberal institutional power restraints (citing Madison). This is surprising because some classical liberals, such as Montesquieu and Hume, discussed both international balance of power and, of course, domestic power restraints. However, they never addressed the two simultaneously, connecting them (e.g., Whelan, 1995).

Of course, Waltz also drew on Hobbesian arguments, including the claim that equality among units in a system leads to greater instability than inequality. Nevertheless, he did not specifically argue for the need to concentrate power in a Leviathan, whether domestic or international.

Despite some liberal inclinations of early realists and their ambiguity regarding Hobbes's influence on their writings, we have come to accept that realism in IR depicts what is essentially a Hobbesian world (Smith, 1986: 13). Indeed, realists have repeatedly referred to Hobbes's parallels between the state of nature among individuals and the state of war between states.

The English School has also drawn upon the Hobbesian notion of the state of nature but distinguished its application to domestic and to international politics, reaching different conclusions than realism. Proponents of this approach have pointed out that Hobbes purposefully did not seek to extend the solution of a Leviathan to the anarchy of the international realm. Scholars such as Vincent (1981) and Bull (1977) argued that this was due to Hobbes's understanding that, although international relations were anarchic, they were not really similar to the state of nature among individuals. In fact, Bull (1981: 732) noted that Hobbes's approach to IR was "deeply pacific."

Other scholars, most prominently Milner (1991), have gone further, and opposed even the notion that the international system is truly anarchic (in great part due to the existence of international law and international institutions), just as domestic systems are not really hierarchic (see also Lake, 2010; Staton and Moore, 2011). Interestingly, this claim has led Milner and others to emphasize the similarities between the international and domestic realms, rather than the differences that had been highlighted by the English School. And, although their arguments parallel those made by realists, to the extent that they note that domestic and international systems are comparable, they depart considerably from them. The realist view is that in both domestic and international systems order can only be established through a government (national or global).[12] Milner's alternative perspective is that there is already a *degree* of order in both domestic and international systems, whether with or without a government maintaining it. Anarchy and hierarchy are best understood as falling at different times and in different systems (either domestic or international) across a continuum, rather than representing two completely opposed concepts (Milner, 1991: 74–76).

The English School and the work of scholars who question the anarchic nature of international politics pushed IR further away from applying Hobbesian arguments to the international realm. Accordingly, while realists may have touched on (but failed to take up) the Lockean argument that once the Hobbesian Leviathan

---

[12] Of course, also through balance of power.

emerges it must be restrained, the English School and other critiques of realism discounted the parallel between the domestic and international Hobbesian worlds altogether and, consequently, passed over arguments related to restraints on power. Most important, none of the existing forms of liberalism has sought to counter the Hobbesian argument for the need of power concentration with the Lockean emphasis on power restraints. Thus, the emergence of realism in IR, strongly based on Hobbes's ideas, created an opportunity to develop a theory that considers the relevance of this essential element of classical liberalism. However, this opportunity was missed throughout most of the Cold War.

Neoliberal Institutionalism: The Influence of Rawls

Immediately after World War II, the stigma associated with interwar foreign policies, which were connected to idealism and liberalism, led to an almost complete "victory" of realism in IR. Scholars showed very little interest in seeking connections either to the IR liberalism of the interwar era or, as noted, to liberal political theory. The tense relations between the United States and USSR, based on nuclear deterrence, that dominated international relations discouraged any such appeal. Moreover, the influence of Waltzian structural realism led to a greater interest in the similarities between the foreign policies of states that were otherwise so different in their domestic attributes.

Two forms of liberalism, however, emerged almost simultaneously in the 1980s in IR theory, countering important realist arguments: neoliberal institutionalism and a revived form of liberal internationalism. Neoliberal institutionalism was sparked in great part by the increase in the number and in the degree of intrusiveness of IGOs toward the end of the Cold War. This phenomenon led IR scholars to question the realist emphasis on interstate conflict and to increasingly turn to studies of cooperation.

Robert Keohane's work was principally responsible for connecting this broader interest in interstate cooperation to liberal political theory. Like other IR scholars over the past few decades, Keohane (1990) acknowledged the varied themes that fall under the broader liberal umbrella. He distinguished three types of liberalism in IR: republican liberalism (the thesis that republics are more peaceful than despotic states), commercial liberalism (the claim that free trade promotes peace), and regulatory liberalism (the argument that international laws and rules support peaceful coexistence). This classification is both similar to and different from the three types of IR liberalism of the interwar era discussed above.[13] Most important, he added to these a fourth type that he labeled "sophisticated liberalism." This

---

[13] The multiple classifications of IR liberalism in the literature are a reflection of the problems that scholars have in distinguishing clearly between the various strands of this theoretical approach.

type, in Keohane's view, combined elements from the other three but also emphasized that interactions among states, especially through trade and international institutions, led states to reconsider their interests, which in turn facilitated greater cooperation. This additional sociological element, focusing on the processes whereby actors reassessed and revised their interests, was behind what he considered to be a more complex (i.e., sophisticated) connection between commerce, international institutions, and peace.

Keohane's work drew heavily from Rawls. He considered that his own approach was "liberal" because it emphasized cooperation between states and processes that stressed "the role of human-created institutions in affecting how aggregations of individuals make collective decisions" (Keohane, 1989: 10), a central Rawlsian theme. While one can argue that cooperative institutional arrangements virtually always have *some* restraining effects on member-states, neoliberal institutionalism made only indirect connections to institutional restraints on power and did not draw upon classical liberalism to explain them.

Keohane's approach paid much greater attention than interwar liberalism to political processes. He explained that his focus on cooperation, defined as a "mutual *adjustment* of interests," distinguished it from harmony, which presupposes that states share common interests before negotiations begin. Therefore, "cooperation," he stressed, "is highly political" (Keohane, 1984: 53). The idea that states change their preferences during the complex processes of cooperation was later developed both by the "new liberal" approach and by alternative theoretical approaches that developed in the 1990s, especially constructivism (e.g., Bearce and Bondanella, 2007; Wendt, 1999).

And yet, some scholars still found neoliberal institutionalism to be *insufficiently political* because, like neorealism, it operated at the system level and therefore was based on some fairly parsimonious assumptions about political interactions. Critics charged that neoliberal institutionalism approached politics as a strategic game between relatively equal rational egoists. They pointed out that this narrow understanding of politics is the result of its focus on the process involved in cooperation, missing much of the outcome of cooperative arrangements (Stein, 2008). Outcomes depend a great deal on the differences in power between the states engaged in strategic games. Its critics contend that neoliberal institutionalism downplays the reality that most solutions emerging from international cooperative processes are in fact imposed by powerful states on weaker ones (see, e.g., Reus-Smit, 2001; Richardson, 2001). In other words, neoliberal institutionalism's lack of attention to power differentials appears to lead it to mischaracterize the political process.

We should stress that, as in the case of interwar liberalism, neoliberal institutionalism cannot be said to completely neglect power restraints.

However, the restraints on power that emerge in a neoliberal institutionalist approach are primarily fortuitous byproducts of the increased ability to cooperate, not as intentionally developed institutional mechanisms seeking to restrain dominant states. Moreover, the limits that cooperative arrangements impose on states' actions do not affect, directly or indirectly, the development of restraints on IGOs themselves, something that, as we will show, recent literature (including Keohane's own subsequent work) has considered more closely. In fact, the cooperation that neoliberal institutionalism emphasizes is the one between great powers. And when great powers come together and agree on common solutions, their ability to impose the resulting IGO policies on small states is even greater than when individual dominant states seek to do so.

Keohane was very much aware of this critique regarding neoliberal institutionalism's relative inattention to power dynamics. Even as early as 1984, he acknowledged that "the principles on which present patterns of cooperation are based show insufficient sensitivity to the interests of disadvantaged people in the Third World" (Keohane, 1984: 256). However, in that earlier writing, he argued that international institutions, even if reflecting power disparities, were nevertheless useful. It was only in his later work, discussed below, that he took up the additional question of how institutions need to be designed to make both states *and* IGOs more accountable for their actions to multiple audiences, including to the many small states (e.g., Keohane, 2001, 2003, 2005). As we will show, this emphasis on accountability has also brought IR liberalism closer than before to questions of institutional power restraints.

Liberal Internationalism and New Liberalism in the 1980s and 1990s

Liberal Internationalism witnessed a resurgence toward the end of the Cold War. An important reason for this revival was the spread of increasingly rigorous statistical analyses supporting the democratic peace argument. While some initial studies were published in the 1960s and 1970s, by the 1980s and 1990s a flurry of tests of this thesis generated a greater interest in the democratic peace finding (e.g., Rummel, 1983; Russett, 1993; Russett et al., 1998; Weede, 1984). A second reason for the revival of liberal internationalism was the rapid increase in the number of democratic polities at the end of the Cold War. Both factors led to a renewed focus on the question of whether democracies behave differently in their interactions with each other compared to their interactions with other states.

Michael Doyle was primarily responsible for connecting the democratic peace findings to liberal political theory. In two articles published in the mid-1980s, Doyle sought to explain both why democracies are peaceful toward each other *and* why they continue to fight wars with nondemocratic states. He noted that, while other authors, such as Machiavelli or Schumpeter, offered partial explanations for the democratic peace, it was primarily the Kantian "tripod" of domestic representative institutions, economic interdependence, and "cosmopolitan right" that best explained why liberal states behaved differently toward each other, compared to other states. Specifically, democratic states allow the general public (that usually bears the costs of wars) to have a voice in domestic and international decisions. The spirit of commerce leads dominant domestic groups in liberal states to have interests in each other's well-being. Cosmopolitan right encourages states to treat each other peaceably.[14] Together, these three legs of the tripod considerably reduce the likelihood of war (Doyle, 1983, 1986).

Although the liberal internationalism that emerged in the 1980s initially focused primarily on the relevance of democracy on interstate relations, influenced by the growing literature testing various facets of the democratic peace findings, academic writings eventually turned to the other two legs of the Kantian tripod: free trade and international institutions (Russett et al., 1998).[15] In the Reagan era, the spread of democracy and free market economies *within states*, as well as free trade *among states*, were promoted simultaneously by Western powers. The next two US administrations of Bush and Clinton also emphasized the importance of international institutions (e.g., Hoffmann, 1995).

In sum, the liberal internationalism of the end of the twentieth century embraced a similar three-pronged approach to IR as the one of the post–World War I era, albeit a purposefully more cohesive one. Once more, one can make the argument that this form of IR liberalism also takes into account questions of restraints on power. However, the restraints prescribed by this scholarship are essentially "internal" ones, those that domestic actors impose on their own governments.

A reflection of liberal internationalism's focus on domestic actors can be found in Doyle's explanation of the process through which such restraints work:

---

[14] We should note that this third leg of the tripod, like the first two, refers primarily to domestic characteristics. The cosmopolitan right Doyle (and Kant) mentions is not the broad restraining type that we usually envision when referring to international law. Rather, it is "limited to conditions of universal hospitality" that further enhance the spirit of commerce (Doyle, 1983: 227).

[15] Indeed, some scholars have built upon the understanding of the liberal internationalist third leg of "cosmopolitan right," presenting it as an argument referring more broadly to international organizations and their restraining role (Russett et al., 1998). We consider this interpretation to be somewhat exaggerated. Doyle (1983: 227) emphasized that the Kantian federation of states does not require institutionalization (e.g., at the basis of the neoliberal institutionalist understanding of international restraints), as Kant appears to have in mind mutual nonaggression pacts or collective security agreements.

> The basic postulate of liberal international theory holds that states have the right to be free from foreign intervention. . . . When states respect each other's rights, individuals are free to establish private international ties without state interference. Profitable exchanges between merchants and educational exchanges among scholars then create a web of mutual advantages and commitments that bolsters sentiments of public respect. (Doyle, 1983: 213)

This excerpt suggests that, for Doyle, territorial integrity, protected by the absence of foreign intervention, opens up space for *citizens* to exercise their political independence, leading to strengthened international ties. In other words, the concentration of power in the hands of one or several states is seen principally as a threat to individuals within states *who seek to interact with each other across borders*. "Foreign intervention" is not understood in terms of the imbalance of power in the international system – the process through which the more powerful states impose their will on *all* citizens of the weaker states. Rather, in Doyle's view, powerful states prevent citizens, their own as well as other states' citizens, who wish to interact (a relatively small number compared to any state's entire population), from doing so.

Not surprisingly, liberal internationalism has been criticized as little more than an ideology that allows the powerful West to impose its will and (liberal) principles on weak states with different ideational traditions (Hoffman, 1995; Reus-Smit, 2001). This was considered a significant oversight even during the Cold War, when such principles openly clashed with those promoted by the powerful Soviet Union and its communist allies. However, in the early Post–Cold War era, when there was no real counterweight to the United States and its Western allies, the liberal internationalist calls for the spread of democracy and market principles to developing states were perceived by some as nothing more than raw projections of neocolonial power (Hall and Hobson, 2010).

Liberal internationalism came under increasing attack in the 1990s as scholars took note of the poverty and military conflicts that raged unabated throughout the world. Its critics underscored the tension between the liberal international call for the spread of *domestic* democratic principles *across* states, and its neglect of inequalities *between* states in the *international* realm. Indeed, small states began calling for the application of "democratic" principles in voting and representation in international institutions such as the UNSC, World Bank, and International Monetary Fund on which great powers had a firm grasp (e.g., Grigorescu, 2015).

Building upon liberalism's various strands in IR, including liberal inter-nationalism and neoliberal institutionalism, Moravcsik (2008) developed a general framework (labeled "new liberalism") to serve as an umbrella for liberal IR theory. His aim was to reformulate "liberal international relations in a nonideological and nonutopian form appropriate to empirical social science" (Moravcsik, 1997: 513). Moravcsik identified three main forms of liberalism in IR: republican, commercial, and ideational. While his first two types of liberalism were identical to Keohane's, the third focused more narrowly on the sociological elements implicit in Keohane's "sophisticated liberalism."

The effort to encompass a fairly broad set of elements under Moravcsik's restatement of liberalism in IR is a result of the maturation of this theoretical approach within the subfield. Compared to earlier IR forms of liberalism, which often sought to explain why they used the "liberal" label, connecting them to the works of political theorists, by the late 1990s when "new liberalism" was developed, there was already a sufficiently rich IR liberal literature to allow Moravcsik to mention only in passing the domestic roots of liberal thought.

Moravcsik's work emphasized the commonalities among *IR* liberalism's various strands. He identified three "core assumptions" underlying all liberal variants: 1) the primacy of societal actors and their preferences for *international relations*; 2) states (*in their interactions*) represent the preferences of some of these societal actors; 3) state behavior is not only the result of such preferences formed through "bottom-up" processes, but also contingent on their interdependence *with other states* in the international system (Moravcsik, 1997). All such assumptions appear to be specific to states and their interactions (as the italicized words suggest) and allow for few and rather vague connections to the interactions between individuals and groups *within* states that was classical liberalism's focus. Perhaps the best indication of new liberalism's very international approach (distinct from liberalism as applied to domestic politics) is what Moravcsik (2008: 234) sees as its "central insight": "The . . . globalization-induced variation in social demands and state preferences is a fundamental cause of state behavior in world politics." This argument is indeed very specific to international interactions and reflects how IR liberalism has come to stand on its own without a need to connect to liberal political theory.

Most important for the present study, while new liberalism is clearly interested in the politics taking place between (and within) states with different preferences and takes power considerations seriously, it does not broach the need to restrain concentrated power. Indeed, none of the three variants of new liberalism, as Moravcsik defines them, or its core assumptions, address the central concern of classical liberal theory – the fear of concentrated power and the development of institutional bulwarks to prevent its arbitrary exercise. In this sense, new liberalism, like virtually all other forms of liberalism in IR, has missed an opportunity to connect to the central theme of classical liberalism as applied to the domestic realm.

The Recent IR Literature on Accountability and Power Restraints: Another Form of Liberalism?

As mentioned earlier, two decades after Keohane outlined the main arguments of neoliberal institutionalism, he sought to expand his narrower focus on IGOs as loci for cooperation and developed a more complete approach that visibly took into account the power asymmetries in international institutions and the necessary mechanisms for holding both states and IGOs accountable (Grant and Keohane, 2005; Keohane, 2001, 2003, 2005; Keohane and Nye, 2002). He portrayed this work as an extension of his neoliberal institutionalist arguments, basing this broader approach on two premises. First, he argued that globalization is leading to increased demands for international institutions. Interestingly, he noted (in a way that recalls the Hobbesian liberals of the interwar era) that although this argument has been associated with liberalism, "it is actually complementary to Hobbes' point" (2001: 1), reflecting an important area of agreement between liberals and realists.[16] Second, drawing on Shklar's "liberalism of fear," he offered a powerful reminder that "international organizations are huge and oppressive . . . seen as serving the vested interests of the powerful and privileged" (Keohane, 2001: 7). He thus concluded his 2000 Presidential Address to the American Political Science Association by arguing that, "As we face globalization, our challenge resembles that of the founding fathers of this country: how to design working institutions for a polity of unprecedented size and diversity" (2001: 12).

Keohane purposefully limited his analogy between the Madisonian (i.e., classical liberal) approach that shaped American institutions and the one that is necessary for designing international institutions, arguing that "it would be quixotic to expect global governance to reach the standards of modern democracies" (2001: 2; see also p. 9). He did not, however, connect the intermingling of Hobbesian (power concentration) and classical liberal (restraints on its inevitable abuse) principles to a realist liberal approach, as we do through a reinterpretation of Locke's writings. "In the liberal democratic tradition that I embrace," he wrote (2001: 9), "voluntary cooperation based on honest communication and rational persuasion provides the strongest guarantee of a legitimate process" of global governance. Thus, he (and Ruth Grant) argued that our main aim should be to promote greater accountability for all international actors, be they states, IGOs, or nongovernmental actors (Grant and Keohane, 2005: 40). Restraints in the international realm were principally

---

[16] As we will show, our focus on Locke's work allows us to emphasize power dynamics in a similar way that Keohane does. Like him we therefore find more common ground with IR realists than scholars from the earlier IR liberal literature.

a product of the successful adoption of norms and processes of accountability, participation, and persuasion (Keohane, 2001: 9–11).

Keohane's (and others') emphasis on IGO accountability was a response to the contemporary context in IR. The end of the Cold War appeared to resolve the gridlock that had kept the UN Security Council from acting when the two major powers would veto each other's initiatives. Throughout the 1990s, the UNSC approved thirty-five new peacekeeping operations, twice as many as in the previous four and a half decades of the UN's existence.[17] The late 1990s, especially the 1997 Asian financial crisis, also showed how the World Bank and IMF had become extraordinarily influential, often stripping small states of their ability to make meaningful decisions, eroding their sovereignty (e.g., Stiglitz, 2003). Last but not least, the 1992 Maastricht Treaty formally established the EU, an institution that came to be much more intrusive for member-states than its precursors. Virtually all states, but especially small ones, began seeing potential dangers in having such active and powerful IGOs and called for mechanisms to hold them accountable.

A series of public protests against powerful IGOs – against the WTO in 1999, against the Bretton Woods institutions on an almost daily basis in the late 1990s in front of their headquarters in Washington DC, and the Danish rejection of the Maastricht Treaty – are reflections of the same broad recognition that IGOs (and not only their member-states) needed to be restrained. This emphasis on IGO accountability constituted a clear break from previous IR literature discussing only restraints on powerful states. Indeed, the IGOs of the turn of the twenty-first century increasingly inched closer to look more like Locke's "lion," certainly much more so than the League, UN, and other major IGOs of the past.

Over the past two decades or so, the literature on IGO accountability (broadly understood as a form of restraint on international institutions) came into its own, with numerous authors discussing in depth specific ways in which accountability could be achieved. Probably the richest such literature focused on the role of transnational actors (especially of NGOs) and their increased ability to keep IGOs and powerful states in check (e.g., Scholte, 2011; Steffek et al., 2008; Tallberg et al., 2013; Willetts, 1996). Numerous works also emphasized the need to make IGOs more transparent to achieve greater accountability (e.g., Florini, 2003). The global constitutionalism literature also included many examples of how international law and judicial institutions could contribute to the accountability of even the most powerful international actors (e.g., Lang and Wiener, 2017).

---

[17] See https://peacekeeping.un.org/sites/default/files/unpeacekeeping-operationlist_3_1_0.pdf.

Others proposed to establish or further develop transnational parliamentary assemblies as a way to achieve greater IGO accountability, restraining both powerful member-states and the IGOs themselves (e.g., Habegger, 2010). Lastly, some works examined new audit, investigation, or inspection offices established starting in the 1990s in many IGOs as internal oversight mechanisms, focusing narrowly on the accountability of IGO secretariats rather than of member-states (e.g., Fox et al., 2000).

More broadly, the rich post–Cold War literature on IGOs has discussed in various ways how power concentration in IGOs (whether it belonged to the dominant states that came together in such organizations or developed independently of them) could be restrained. Most obviously, powerful states themselves held IGOs accountable and restrained their actions (e.g., Grant and Keohane, 2005). Additionally, the fragmentation of IGO authority across issues and geographic areas established some checks and balances *between* various organizations in a similar way as institutions from different branches of government constituted checks on each other (e.g., Möllers, 2013). Yet others noted how the increasing tensions between international law and domestic law are leading to a "pluralist" approach that establishes checks in both realms (e.g., Krisch, 2010).

Michael Zürn's broad body of work, especially *A Theory of Global Governance* (2018), has made multiple connections between the disparate elements of this scholarship. He argued that world politics unfolds in normative and institutional structures that reflect power asymmetries. Such structures are in a continuous quest for legitimization that, in turn, leads to politicized processes of contestation within and of international institutions. Zürn thus joined the growing scholarship emphasizing both power considerations and political processes in international institutions and underscoring some of the deficiencies of existing liberal IR theories that have not paid sufficient attention to these two elements.[18] Moreover, when discussing contestation, not surprisingly, Zürn touched upon processes that restrained power (both of dominant states and of international institutions that he saw as having themselves come to hold political sway), especially those that give a voice to smaller states, civil society organizations, courts, and even public opinion. However, even this comprehensive work does not make the direct connection between the three Lockean elements we discuss in this Element and the important *balance* between them. Moreover, Zürn generally does not dwell on *institutional* restraints on power, as those emphasized by Locke and the classical liberals,

---

[18] Specifically, he argued that his book "aims to demolish the seemingly unbreakable elective affinity between institutionalism and a cooperative reading of world politics" (2018: 3).

but rather on those based on the strategic use of international norms in contestation processes.

Overall, this broad recent body of literature on accountability and political contestation[19] has clear synergies with classical liberalism. However, like new liberalism, it has not made explicit connections to classical liberal writings and to their essential focus on institutional power restraints. Moreover, this scholarship is still fairly amorphous, with few efforts to synthesize it as a whole. We suggest that a Lockean (or classical liberal) approach to IR could bring together many of these works that focus primarily on the accountability of and restraints on states and the increasingly influential IGOs, as well as other works mentioned above.

Two Recent Bodies of IR Theory Directly Focusing on Power Restraints

In addition to the IR literature on accountability, a handful of other works has engaged more directly with questions related to restraints on the power both of dominant states and of IGOs. Daniel Deudney specifically underscored the need to develop institutional restraints on power in the international context. His work focused on the problem of "liberty dealing with power" (Deudney, 2007: 280, n. 9). "Security from political violence," he argued, is "the first freedom, the minimum vital task of all primary political associations" (Deudney, 2007: 14). He noted that both domestic and international politics must find a solution to the threat of "violence interdependence, a rough and basic measure of the capacity of actors to wreak destruction upon one another," posed by both extreme anarchy *and* extreme hierarchy (Deudney, 2007: 18). He did not, however, trace ways of addressing these two "extremes" to Hobbesian and Lockean roots. Rather, he subsumed them under what he saw as a much older tradition of "republican security theory." In his view, liberalism and realism are "children" of republicanism and only incompletely embraced the main tenets of the original theoretical approach (Deudney, 2007: 15).[20]

Deudney (2007: 37–41) sought a way to resolve the threat of *international* violence without yielding to *domestic* despotism. In his view, the US founding

---

[19] Much of this literature was produced by European scholars who reacted not only to global changes but also to the extraordinary increase in the EU's power.

[20] We should not exaggerate, however, the distinction between Deudney's use of the "republican" tradition and our use of the "liberal" one. There is an extensive literature on the historical relationship between republicanism and liberalism. Like Deudney, we are persuaded by scholars who distinguish between classical and "modern" (Pangle, 1988) or "new" (Zuckert, 1994) republicanism. The latter refers to regimes that embody the values of "political liberty, popular sovereignty, and limited government" (Deudney, 2007: 5), precisely the core of the liberal tradition of political theory.

formed a pivotal moment for this project: the American republic solved the problem of ameliorating anarchy over progressively larger geographical areas without resorting to a hierarchical state (despotism or empire) (Deudney, 2007: 161–85). He acknowledged that the United States projected its power through IGOs such as the League and the UN, but he argued that such liberal IGOs can serve to limit the development of domestic hierarchy in response to the threat of international anarchy (Deudney, 2007: 185–89). In contrast, our focus is on the challenge of international *hierarchy*, that is, on the efforts by smaller powers to develop mechanisms through international institutions to constrain the more powerful states, including the United States, as well as to constrain the IGOs themselves.

Last but not least, John Ikenberry, an author whose work shaped the liberal internationalist literature discussed earlier, is one of the few scholars who discusses head-on the questions of *institutional* restraints on power through IGOs. In *After Victory* (2001), he argued that after major conflicts states reach "constitutional bargains" through which the hegemonic power is able to impose a predictable and legitimate international order in exchange for its acceptance of restraints on the use of power. While this argument approximates the classical liberal understanding of how and why institutional restraints on power emerge, it offers only a partial explanation primarily because its focus is almost entirely on the role of the most powerful state and its *voluntary* acceptance of "fences" (the United Kingdom and in the nineteenth century and the United States in the twentieth century) (see Deudney and Ikenberry, 2021; Ikenberry 2011). By doing so, it downplays the concerns and actions of weak actors, who often see all concentrations of power as a problem, something that, as we show, is classical liberalism's essential lesson.

Conclusions

The above survey of the literature suggests that IR theory has frequently drawn from multiple elements of liberal political theory. Yet the liberalism that has resulted in IR has been shaped in great part by scholars seeking to develop a counterweight to the dominant realist paradigm and has been tailored to suit the main concerns of each period, such as the outbreak of world wars, waves of democratization, or the spread (and later empowerment) of IGOs (Richardson, 2001). The development of liberalism as a complex body of scholarship in political theory has allowed IR theory to seek only specific elements to serve the fairly narrow purposes of the moment. As shown, this cherry-picking approach sometimes led to the neglect of politics and power considerations (thus leaving very little common ground between IR liberalism and realism). And it virtually always neglected the essential original theme of classical liberals starting with Locke, the need to restrain concentrated power.

We noted that the opportunities to focus on power restraints were always present. Yet, when IR literature recently began addressing restraints, especially through accountability mechanisms, the links to classical liberal theory were neglected. Liberal internationalism has also come close to taking the Lockean notion of restraints on concentrated power seriously but, each time, has stopped short. Starting with Kant's arguments and moving along through those underlying the liberal internationalist Western foreign policies going back to Woodrow Wilson, we can find evidence of the basic idea that the weak need to be protected through mechanisms that restrain the powerful. However, the nature of restraints on power considered by liberal internationalism is narrow. It is the public within the dominant state that can use such restraints against their own powerful leaders. And, of course, such a public is likely to have a very different interest (and reasons to restrain its leaders) than the ones from other states. In other words, while liberal internationalism accounts for restraints on international power *within* states, it downplays the need for similar restraints *among* states.[21]

Classical liberal theorists responded to the challenge of restraining the concentration of power in the modern state by introducing institutional mechanisms such as the rule of law, separation of powers, federalism, and the various mechanisms for holding the institutions of government accountable. Our interpretation of Locke and of classical liberalism will allow us to show how his political theory offers valuable insights for understanding better the international realm, especially through his strong emphasis on political processes and power considerations (what we consider to be two elements of his "tripod"), in addition to his well-known focus on power restraints (the third element), and thus leads to a balanced approach that complements existing forms of IR liberalism as well as other IR theories.

2 John Locke's Realist Liberal Tripod

Locke's Realist Liberalism

That Locke's political theory is centrally shaped by realist considerations is scarcely self-evident.[22] Locke's appeal to universal principles of natural law

---

[21] Locke was aware of the potential problems deriving from domestic restraints on international power. It is hardly unreasonable to envisage situations, he argues (2.188), in which "all the Men of [a] Community being all Members of the same Body Politick, may be taken to have joyn'd in [an] unjust War."

[22] We tease out the "realist" dimensions of Locke's liberalism and, more generally, of the classical liberal tradition, from the realist critique of John Rawls that emerged in political theory in the

and equal rights, the state of nature, and the social contract is antithetical to the sensibilities of a realist approach to politics (Bell, 2014: 695–96 and n. 57). His own contemporaries, Locke conceded, charged him with ignoring the historical reality "That there are no Instances to be found in Story of a Company of Men independent and equal one amongst another, that met together, and in this way began and set up a Government" (2.100). In contrast to most Whig thinkers, who scoured England's ancient constitution to justify their opposition to Charles II's moves to consolidate power in his hands, Locke's political theory appealed to normative principles of natural right.[23]

Locke's political theory is not, however, the work of an abstract thinker, detached from historical experience and the realities of power politics. The argument of the "Second Treatise" is informed by historical accounts of peoples' lives under various governments and the lessons they drew from them (2.103). Locke's is a hybrid political theory, writes Ashcraft (1987: 98), "composed of two distinguishable parts, one rooted in moral principles and the other in prudential judgments based upon experience" (see Grant, 1987: 48–51). The "Second Treatise" was in part a call to arms, an effort to engage the emotions and energies of fellow Whigs "to examine more carefully the Original and Rights of Government; and to find out ways to restrain the Exorbitances, and prevent the Abuses" of the monarch's power (2.111). "The persuasive force of Locke's specific political objectives," explains Ashcraft (1987: 98), depended "on the ability of Locke's contemporary readers to recognize that 'the state all men are

---

1990s. Williams (2005) is often cited as the founder of this realist approach. We stress that, although they may share some concerns, realism in political theory developed independently of and is distinct from realism in IR. For analyses of the realist approach in political theory, see Galston (2010); Sager (2016); Sleat (2011); Stears (2007). Although the literature is now extensive, realists are distinguished by a common set of guiding principles. Their starting point is a frank acknowledgment of the ineradicable differences among human beings about the ends of social life. Political conflict is in their view ubiquitous, and they reject the claim that an appeal to moral principles can resolve our social dissensus. Rather, realists accept that conflict is ineliminable and seek ways to manage it. Coercion and politics play constitutive roles in creating and stabilizing social institutions. First, realists acknowledge that the concentration of coercive power is necessary to underwrite cooperation. Second, they argue that "the core challenge of politics is to overcome anarchy without embracing tyranny" (Galston, 2010: 391). Politics involves practices of negotiation and accommodation and institutional mechanisms of accountability and redress that restrain the concentration of power and civilize conflict. Realist political theorists have not reexamined the political theory of Locke or classical liberalism. Their approach, however, provides us with the conceptual framework guiding our reinterpretation of Locke's and the classical liberals' understanding of politics and power.

[23] The Whig party formed during the Exclusion Controversy (1679–1681), a political effort to check the power of Charles II and to exclude his brother James II from succeeding to the English throne. Whigs charged that Charles endeavored to concentrate power in the monarchy modeled on the absolutist rule of Louis XIV of France. For the political differences between Locke and the moderate Whigs, see Ashcraft (1986: 27–33, 176); Ashcraft (1987: 25–34). For the theoretical differences between them, see Zuckert (1994: 97–149, 289–91). See also Tully (1993: 12, 19, 42–44).

naturally in' is deeply rooted in the experience of their own life-world" (see also Tully, 1993: 21–22, 33–34).

In this section, we maintain that commentators have offered an unbalanced account of the "two distinguishable parts" of Locke's political theory, overstating its normative principles at the expense of its realist dimensions (e.g., Ashcraft, 1987: 156; Grant, 1987: 27–51, 179–92; Tuckness, 2002: 181–89; Zuckert, 1994: 272–78). Our aim is to rectify this imbalance – to disentangle and establish the constitutive role of politics and power, in addition to his overriding concern to restrain power, in his work. Locke attests that the law of nature does exist and ought to guide us but nonetheless adopts a realist approach to politics. The reason is that, in his view, human beings have scant capacity to agree upon or to live by moral principles, and especially to apply them to their circumstances. Locke is too keen and too honest an observer of human psychology and history to conclude that human beings can achieve a widely shared normative consensus, prior to politics, to direct the practical task of constructing rules to guide their cooperation. His acknowledgement of the natural law's limits in creating social order marks the threshold to his realism. The commands of natural law only establish the challenge of politics; organizing a government is an acutely fraught process that must be worked out by negotiation and accommodation predicated on an understanding of power and politics.

Although they differed from each other and from Locke, classical liberals – Montesquieu, Kant, and the authors of *The Federalist* – also tempered their normative commitments with a realist approach to politics. We shall argue that the realist dimensions of classical liberalism consist in the following claims: human dissensus, including disagreements about the interpretation of our moral obligations, is ubiquitous and ineradicable. The only way a group of individuals succeeds in containing their endemic disputes short of violence is by taking up the practices of politics, which must include all individuals if they are to be persuaded to give up the recourse to force. The state, with the monopoly over the legitimate exercise of coercion, is necessary to create and maintain order. The danger that rulers and powerful groups will arbitrarily use the power in their hands establishes the central task of politics – designing institutional mechanisms to restrain their power and lift the burden of fear from the people they rule. Theirs is, to borrow Shklar's words (1989: 27), a "liberalism of fear."[24]

---

[24] Shklar (1989: 21) contends that the liberalism of fear captures "the original and only defensible meaning of liberalism." Yet she distances her version from classical versions, including Locke's, which are "given to hope" (Shklar, 1989: 27; see also 23–24, 26–27). Yet see Shklar (1984: 226–49), where, while still distinguishing them, she draws a much closer connection between classical liberalism and the liberalism of fear.

The principal source of fear is "the inevitability of that inequality of military, police, and persuasive power which is called government . . . . And the freedom it wishes to secure is freedom from the abuse of power and intimidation of the defenseless that this difference invites." We conclude that these three elements – politics, power, and restraints on power – form a tripod, each "leg" relying on and balancing the others, through which liberal order is created and maintained.

We turn first to Locke's reflections on international relations. As commentators have noted, Locke's discussion of this topic is thin. "International relations," writes Ward (2006: 691), "were not the primary focus of his work, and foreign affairs is treated less systematically by Locke than other modern political philosophers such as Machiavelli, Grotius, and Kant." Nevertheless, we show that his discussion frames the problem we address – the fear of dangerous concentrations of power and the need to curtail its abuse.

Locke on International Relations

The state of nature is in Locke's view a permanent feature of international relations. He does not envisage anything like a global government, or even international organizations, to secure or promote cooperation: commonwealths, unlike individuals, "ever will be" in a natural state (2.14; see also 2.91, 2.145, 2.181, 2.184). Interpretations of Locke's approach to international politics rely, following Locke, on an analogy between the domestic and international states of nature. Scholars have offered three different views. First, one group of commentators presents Locke as an early modern realist, in the tradition established by Machiavelli and Hobbes, predicated on his view that the law of nature, which spells out our moral obligations, fails to restrain powerful states or pacify intense international rivalries (Cox, 1960; Pangle and Ahrensdorf, 1999: 153–57). A second group of scholars takes Locke's moral commitments seriously. Drawing on his view that states, like individuals, have a duty to enforce the law of nature, they maintain that Locke sanctions an expansive internationalism, including interference in a delinquent state's internal affairs (Seliger, 1969: 114–18; Simmons, 1992: 127–34; Ward, 2006: 692, 694–95, 701–03). Third, Locke's defense of commercial expansion is the basis of an interpretation that he provided a justification of the English colonial project (Arneil, 1996; Tuck, 1999: 173–78; Tully 1993: 137–76). These interpretations all suggest that Locke's portrait of the international realm is especially violent – oscillating between armed conflict and uneasy peace – whether because states routinely ignore or violate moral norms or, alternatively, because moral norms authorize violence, against other states or against indigenous peoples.

Our view builds upon, but in significant ways departs from, these interpretations. Locke is indeed a realist: his shrewd understanding of human psychology and history underlies a deep pessimism regarding the capacities of human beings, and especially their governments, to comply with their moral obligations or to agree on principles of peaceful coexistence. The law of nature prohibits aggression, but Locke acknowledges that its obligations fail to maintain international order or peace (2.175, 2.176, 2.179, 2.180, 2.184, 2.11). To the contrary, not only do aggressor states enlist the law of nature to justify their depredations, they are "rewarded with Laurels and Triumphs, because they are too big for the weak hands of Justice in this World, and have the power in their own possession, which should punish Offenders" (2.176; also 2.179). Moreover, because every state has the power to interpret the law of nature (2.145), the absence of agreement among them contributes to international conflict. Nevertheless, Locke's principal aim is to find ways of taming the anarchic character of international relations by turning to politics as the principal alternative to war. Political negotiation and accommodation open possibilities for international cooperation.

Locke's discussion of the international state of nature is organized around power asymmetries: his main fear is the irresistible temptation of "the strong and powerful" states to grasp at power and enlarge their possessions by engaging in acts of aggression against their weaker neighbors (2.180; also 2.176, 2.179, 2.184, 2.186). Governments, much like single individuals, possess the natural right to "appeal to heaven," that is, to defend their claims and enforce international obligations on the field of battle (2.176). Enforcement of the law of nature, in the international as in the domestic realm, extends beyond self-defense to include punishment and deterrence, ranging from a demand for reparations (2.181–83) to lawful conquest (2.177, 2.179, 2.183, 2.196). Yet Locke's realism registers substantial prudential warnings against a robust internationalism. He cautions that, in his "appeals to Heaven," a ruler "must be sure he has Right on his side; and a Right too that is worth the Trouble and Cost of the Appeal" (2.176). The rhetoric of law enforcement is more likely to provide support for the "Great Robbers" to "punish little ones, to keep them in their Obedience" (2.176; also 2.179, 2.180, 2.184). Locke questions whether even democratic governments are less prone to violate natural law, envisioning situations in which "all the Men of that Community being all Members of the same Body Politick, may be taken to have join'd" in an unjust war (2.188).

Locke's chief aim, in the international as in the domestic domain, is to find ways of restraining powerful states. His most extended discussion of international relations involves an effort to limit the rights of conquerors, including lawful conquerors, over the defeated populations.[25] As we have seen, however, weaker states are largely defenseless against powerful ones. To defeated peoples, subject to the injustices of the more powerful, Locke's counsel amounts to little more than "patience" (2.176; also 2.196). Only economic development can provide states with the demographic and military strength that will render them "too hard for [their] neighbours" (2.42).

In Locke's view, however, the recourse to force is not the only response available to governments. Two principles begin to distinguish Locke's from Machiavelli's and Hobbes's realism: first, he anticipates the view, made famous by Montesquieu and Kant, that relations among states can be pacified by channeling military rivalries into commercial competition (1.33, 2.42, 2.192; see Pangle and Ahrensdorf, 1999: 154, 156–57; Zuckert, 1994: 262–72, 307–08).[26] Second, and more importantly, he opens room for politics as the principal alternative for resolving conflicts short of war. For Locke, the normative core of international relations is each political community's indefeasible right to work out its own domestic political arrangements (2.190–92). Territorial integrity is the single most consequential principle promoting international order (2.45). But only negotiations among governments can begin to resolve the massive disagreements that beset their international relations. Politics comprises the practices and institutions through which governments work out, "by common Consent," the norms and expectations that are "wanting" in the state of nature (2.45, 2.124). Bargaining and reciprocal agreements, concluding in "Leagues and Alliances" (2.146; also 2.14, 2.45), build trust among governments, mitigating their fear that compliance will only expose them to violence (Grant, 1987: 113–14).[27] Especially important for Locke are "the Leagues that have been made between several States and Kingdoms, either expressly or tacitly disowning all Claim and Right to the Land in the others Possession, ... and so have, by positive agreement, settled a Property amongst themselves, in distinct Parts and parcels of the Earth"

---

[25] "Second Treatise," Chapter XVI, "Of Conquest." No conquering state, however just its cause, is morally authorized to punish noncombatants among the defeated population, especially women and children (2.182–83); entitled to any property in the defeated commonwealth beyond the funds required for reparations (2.180, 2.184); or, most importantly, can its conquest be understood to establish the basis for a legitimate government without the free consent of the conquered populations (2.186–87). Locke's strictures on the rights of conquerors suggest possible limits on any justification of colonialism (see Ward, 2006: 700–01).

[26] Montesquieu (1949 [1748]: XX.1–2.316–17, XXI.20.364–66) and Kant (1991 [1795]: 114) maintained that commercial growth made war more costly because it disrupted potential gains from trade. Montesquieu's *Spirit of the Laws* (1949 [1748]) is hereafter cited book, chapter(s), and page number(s).

[27] Locke argues that compliance with contracts is a moral imperative (2.14, 2.194, 2.195). But he distinguishes between the moral force of obligations and the practical reasons for complying with them under particular circumstances. Compliance with our moral obligations is predicated on the expectation that it will not expose us to another's predatory conduct (2.176, 2.186). See also Dunn (1984: 288–89).

(2.45; also 2.38). A state's jurisdictional claims within a given territory carry an implicit renunciation of territorial claims against other states. Moreover, international agreements – for example, to establish commercial or diplomatic relations – imply mutual recognition among states and a formal acknowledgement of their equal membership in an international society. Finally, recognition of the territorial principle supplies a conventional definition of aggression in international relations, establishing "a basis for self-defense and collective security arrangements" (Ward, 2006: 699). Yet, Locke's realism tempers any optimism that mere leagues and alliances will curb the abuse of power in international relations. States may be morally and legally equal, but they are materially unequal, and Locke acknowledges that international agreements will have scant success in restraining the more powerful states from having their way (2.175, 2.176, 2.179, 2.180, 2.184, 2.11; see Cox, 1960: 165–71; Ward, 2006: 704).

One of our central claims is that a Lockean approach that addresses power concentration in the international realm must rely on an analogy to the tripod of principles – politics, power, and restraints on power – he develops in his analysis of the domestic realm. We turn, then, to Locke's realist liberalism, and to the contributions of classical liberals, to draw the principles that will help to bring together disparate approaches to IR, and to open new avenues of research.

Social Dissensus

The state's monopoly of organized violence, in Locke's view, poses the central problem of politics, because it consists of the power to harm (2.20, 2.107, 2.111, 2.201). The aims of his "Second Treatise," then, are to explain why coercion is necessary in human affairs; to distinguish legitimate from illegitimate forms of political coercion; and to encourage resistance against its illegitimate forms. Justifying the origins and proper end of government takes Locke to the state of nature, a reconstruction of people's lives without government to adjudicate their disputes (2.19). The state of nature spells out Locke's liberal moral commitments – his conception of every person's equal natural right to life, liberty, and estates (2.4, 2.87, 2.123), and their natural law obligations, derived from God's command not "to harm another in his Life, Health, Liberty, or Possessions" (2.6).

Locke maintains that the law of nature is "intelligible and plain to a rational Creature," indeed "possibly plainer" than "the positive Laws of Commonwealths" (2.12; also 2.135). Wanton trespasses of natural law place aggressors in a state of war with their victims and indeed with all humankind (2.8, 2.11, 2.16–20). The moral structure of Locke's argument is predicated on a demonstrable distinction between the state of nature and war. In contrast to Hobbes (1994 [1651]: XIII.3–11), who characterized humans' natural state as a condition of war, involving the ready use of violence to settle controversies, Locke draws a sharp line between them (2.19).[28] Rightful force is permissible only to punish its wrongful use.

Locke's normative commitments, however, exist in an uneasy tension with his political realism. The shared interpretation of natural law that underlies his moral framework quickly disintegrates in practice. Locke cautions that the law of nature is evident to "all . . . who will but consult it" (2.6; also 2.124, 2.136). In a realist vein, drawing on his pessimistic assessment of people's capacities and motivations, he concludes that conflict in the state of nature is pervasive, and he is none too sanguine about the possibility of achieving a normative consensus to ameliorate it (see Zuckert, 1994: 234–37). Locke distinguishes two sources of conflict. He initially identifies "aggressors" as the principal threat to peace (2.16–20). War is the product of "the corruption, and vitiousness of degenerate Men" (2.128), who reject "the ties of the Common Law of Reason, have no other Rule, but that of Force and Violence, and so may be treated as Beasts of Prey" (2.16). Only the organized efforts of morally motivated individuals can restrain aggressors. Yet it is precisely these efforts at concerted action that appeals to our moral obligations fail to secure. As his argument develops, Locke identifies, and underscores, a second source of conflict: our profound dissensus over the terms of the natural law. Conflicts generated by aggressors and conflicts grounded in moral disagreement have different, indeed incompatible, sources: whereas aggressors lack or have deficient moral motivations, our normal moral motivations exacerbate the conflict caused by disagreement. The source of our conflicts is the very appeal to natural law that is intended to resolve them (Barrett, 2020: 334–54).

Locke begins with the realist observation that the natural law is ineffectual without external coercion (2.7). Aggressors present a special difficulty: no one individual, however much "he . . . has right on his side, having ordinarily but his own single strength, hath . . . force enough to defend himself from Injuries, or to punish Delinquents" (2.136). Locke offers two ways whereby aggressors may be repelled. First, he enjoins everyone to engage in collective action to enforce the natural law's commands. Locke authorizes every individual to undertake vigilante action – to judge, execute the judgment, and to seek reparations – against anyone who violates natural law (2.7–12, 2.16). Vigilante justice in the state of nature is necessary to maintain peace: the aggressor "renders himself liable to be destroied by the injur'd person and the rest of mankind, that will joyn him in the execution of Justice" (2.172).

---

[28] Hobbes's *Leviathan* (1994 [1651]) is hereafter cited chapter(s) and paragraph number(s).

Second, Locke authorizes extravagant leaps in the scope and degree of morally permissible punishments (Simmons, 1992: 130–31). In principle, he countenances only punishment proportional to the crime (2.8). Yet proportional punishment proves inadequate to maintain peace. Realist considerations press him to authorize punishment, or its threat, "to such a Degree, as may hinder" the violation of the natural law, beyond any limits defined by restraint or reparation (2.7). He insists that it is "Lawful for a Man to kill a Thief, who has not in the least hurt him . . . any farther then by the use of Force, so to get him in his Power, as to take away his Money, or what he pleases from him" (2.18). Only an expansive use of deterrence renders the law of nature effective: "Each Transgression," argues Locke, "may be punished to that degree, and with so much Severity as will suffice to make it an ill bargain to the Offender, give him cause to repent, and terrifie others from doing the like" (2.12).

Neither the obligation to join others in enforcing the law of nature nor deterrence, however, succeeds in ensuring mutual security (2.127). Aggressors are not the only or even the principal disruptors of peace. The underlying obstacle to peaceful coexistence is the massive dissensus among human beings over their interpretation and application of the natural law's obligations:

> That in such a great variety of traditions, warring among themselves, it would be impossible to establish what the law of nature is, difficult even to judge what is true, what false; what is law, what opinion; what nature commands, what interest, what reason persuades us of, what civil society teaches. Since, indeed, traditions everywhere are so varied, men's opinions so manifestly contradictory and in conflict with one another, not only in different nations, but within the same state; [and since] every opinion we learn from others is "tradition," [and], finally, since each contends so fiercely for his own opinion and demands that he be believed, it would be impossible to know what that "tradition" is or to choose the truth in such a great variety. (Locke, 1990 [1664]: folios 28–29; also folios 17, 66, 68–71)[29]

Quarrels in the state of nature are often defined by situations in which both parties appeal to irreconcilable interpretations of natural law. Both consider themselves innocent, both unjustly injured, so that "every the least difference" between them, Locke acknowledges, "is apt to end" in war (2.21). Dissensus frustrates collective efforts to enforce natural law. Moreover, because all individuals, "through Passion or Interest shall mis-cite, or misapply" the law of

---

[29] Locke's view that "in all Collections of Men," the "variety of Opinions, and contrariety of Interests . . . unavoidably" frustrate agreement on their moral obligations is one of his considered conclusions (2.98). See also Locke's *An Essay Concerning Human Understanding* (1975 [1689]): I.3.6, II.21.54–56, IV.20.1 (hereafter cited Book, Chapter(s), and Section number(s)); Ashcraft (1987: 55); Zuckert (1994: 198–99).

nature (2.136), they are "very apt" to carry punishment "too far, and with too much heat, in their own Cases," so that deterrence escalates into "Revenge" (2.125). Vigilante justice invites cycles of reprisal that destroy confidence that the law of nature will be observed or can be enforced. The duty to obey its commands is undermined by what human beings can realistically expect of one another; aggression or the fear of aggression voids our obligations (2.176, 2.186).

The "appeal to heaven" – every individual's right to enforce the natural law as they interpret it – is now, rather than a necessary condition for the enjoyment of rights, the cause of general insecurity and fear.[30] Our obligations under natural law not only fail to pacify mutual relations, they aggravate conflict. The erosion of trust, driven by the "irregular and uncertain" (2.127) execution of the natural law, overwhelms the state of nature, creating a condition that is "full of fears and continual dangers" (2.123). Coupled with Locke's observations regarding human partiality, the individual right to punish makes the state of nature as insecure as Hobbes's: enjoyment of the natural rights to one's own person and estate, in the state of nature, "is very uncertain, and constantly exposed to the Invasion of others." Life, "however free," is "very unsafe, very unsecure" (2.123; also 2.124–25, 2.127, 2.136).

The inescapability of social discord frames the main political challenge of the "Second Treatise": establishing a common judge to adjudicate disputes. Hence its central question: "who shall be Judge?" (2.21, 2.240–41. See Grant, 1987: 179; Tully, 1993: 20). Hobbes (1994 [1651]: XVII-XVIII) had resolved the dilemma by concentrating all political power in the sovereign. Because no consensus in the state of nature was possible, only a final authority could decide all controversies among subjects. Hobbes's sovereign was thus absolute, above domestic law and beyond recall. Locke's interpreters have struggled to identify his departure from Hobbes's political prescription. The clearest distinction appears to lie in Locke's normative principles. Zuckert (1994: 277) argues that, "even if in the state of nature it is difficult, if not impossible, to distinguish rightful from wrongful violence in practice, it nonetheless remains true in principle that gratuitous harm to others is wrong." Zuckert, however, restates

---

[30] For Locke's understanding of the "appeal to heaven," see 2.20, 2.21, 2.168, 2.176, 2.224, 2.241, 2.242. Locke's audience would have recognized the system of natural adjudication as "a fairly accurate description of the accusatory system of justice by which Europeans governed themselves until the legal revolution of the twelfth and thirteenth centuries . . . . The accusatory system was supplanted by institutionalized and fiscalized forms of juridical government roughly during the reign of Henry II and it was officially banned throughout Europe at the fourth Lateran Council of 1215 . . . . The most important technique . . . is . . . a 'trial by battle' or combat, understood as an 'appeal to heaven' . . . on the assumption that God would judge through the battle's outcome" (Tully, 1993: 21).

the practical difficulty: how do human beings, as Locke portrays them, work out an agreement to end their ubiquitous conflicts? How do they solve the problem that bedevils them in the state of nature, where violence is the ready answer to "every the least" disagreement (2.21)?

The profound discord among human beings over rival terms of cooperation forms the starting point of classical liberal thought. For Kant (1991 [1797]: 137), as for Locke, the state of nature is a Hobbesian condition wherein "human beings act in a violent and malevolent manner, and ... they tend to fight among themselves until an external coercive legislation supervenes" (also Kant, 1991 [1784]: 44–45, [1795]: 112–13; Waldron, 2006: 189). Similarly, in *Federalist* 10 (1961 [1788]: 58–59), Madison maintained that "the latent causes of faction are ... sown in the nature of man .... [H]uman passions have ... divided mankind into parties, inflamed them with mutual animosity, and rendered them much more disposed to vex and oppress each other, than to co-operate for their common good" (also *Federalist* 1: 4–5, *Federalist* 6: 28–29, *Federalist* 51: 349; Epstein, 1984: 68–71). Moreover, like Locke, these classical liberals claimed that moral norms are simply too weak to restrain human passions and ambitions (Kant, 1991 [1784]: 46; Montesquieu, 1949 [1748]: XI.4.150; *Federalist* 10, 1961 [1788]: 61). Individual liberty only exacerbates the problem because, as Kant (1991 [1784]: 44) put it, everyone "encounters in himself the unsocial characteristic of wanting to direct everything in accordance with his own ideas" (see also *Federalist* 10, 1961 [1788]: 58). Nevertheless, to adopt Hobbes's absolute sovereign because it suppresses discord, writes Madison, is to offer a "remedy ... worse than the disease." Not only does tyranny violate natural rights, it is also, he wrote, echoing Locke (2.93, 2.137), foolish: "but it could not be a less folly to abolish liberty, which is essential to *political* life, because it nourishes faction, than it would be to wish the annihilation of air, which is essential to animal life, because it imparts to fire its destructive agency" (*Federalist* 10, 1961 [1788]: 58 (emphasis added); see Epstein, 1984: 67–68; also Kant 1991 [1792]: 84–85, [1795]: 112–13, 125; Montesquieu 1949 [1748]: XIX.27.307–310).

Why is political life so critical to social order? The answer, we shall now argue, is that the liberty to engage in politics is the principal alternative to the violence of the state of nature. Or, to return to Locke, to rectify the "many things wanting" in nature – coming to an agreement on a "common measure to decide all Controversies between them" – individuals must first relinquish their appeal to natural law and agree to resolve their differences politically (2.124). Locke defines power as the jurisdictional authority to judge (2.3, 2.91). And the answer to the question – who shall be judge? – is a *political* one.

Politics

The natural law has a decidedly limited political reach. Locke notes that "the Obligations of the Law of Nature, cease not in Society, but only in many Cases are drawn closer," given specific legal forms and sanctions (2.135). Their challenge, however, is that no authoritative interpretation of its commands is available to them when human beings turn to negotiate the terms of their political association. Immediately following this section, Locke cautions that "the Law of Nature being unwritten, and so no where to be found but in the minds of Men, they who through Passion or Interest shall mis-cite, or misapply it, cannot so easily be convinced of their mistake where there is no establish'd Judge: And so it serves not, as it ought, to determine the Rights, and fence the Properties of those that live under it, especially where every one is Judge, Interpreter, and Executioner of it too, and that in his own Case" (2.136).

Locke accepts our pervasive dissensus and seeks to civilize it by persuading contentious individuals that it is in their interest to replace reprisals with politics. He contends that putting an end to vigilante justice and the cycles of retaliation and escalation in which it traps them requires individuals to "give up all their Natural Power to the Society which they enter into" (2.136; see also 2.87, 2.88, 2.127, 2.131, 2.171). This move is normally interpreted as a necessary step to authorize a government. Equally important, however, it represents Locke's effort to encourage individuals to *forbear* from making the appeal to heaven, temper their moral claims against one another, and turn to politics. Joining a political association, resigning to the commonwealth the power to protect their disparate interests, requires every individual to overcome his fear "that Self-love will make Men partial to themselves and their Friends. And ... that Ill Nature, Passion and Revenge will carry them too far in punishing others" (2.13). No appeal to the law of nature can allay their fears; moral indignation is one of the principal drivers of their controversies (2.19–21). Yet no association can endure unless its members learn to trust that they will not be taken advantage of – that they can safely relinquish their natural powers and work out a publicly acknowledged "Standard of Right and Wrong" unavailable in the state of nature (2.124; also 2.131, 2.171). They must acknowledge their disagreements and manage the mess that bedevils them (Locke, 1975 [1689]: I.1.2–3, IV.14.2, 3, IV.15.4).

Trust is predicated on their willingness to engage in the mutual adjustment of their rival interests.[31] On the one hand, to "wholly" relinquish the power to punish entails abandoning the use of violence to settle their disputes (2.1). "And this is done by barely agreeing to unite into one Political Society, which is all the Compact that is, or needs be, between the Individuals, that enter into, or make

---

[31] See Dunn (1984) for an analysis of Locke's understanding of the complex problem of trust.

up, a Common-wealth" (2.99). On the other, to "give up" the appeal to heaven entails the recognition that various terms of cooperation are conducive to their common preservation, that no agreement amongst them embodies an authoritative or definitive interpretation of natural law, and that insisting on any one interpretation – "obstinacy" or "stiffness" in holding on to their opinions (Locke, 1975 [1689]: IV.16.3) – only serves to sow discord.[32] Politics can begin only when they cease pretending that the law of nature determines or can determine what must be done. The alternatives to politics are war or tyranny – or, more likely, war that leads to tyranny. Their mutual forbearance facilitates and sustains politics (Locke, 1975 [1689]: IV.14.2, IV.16.4).[33]

Because there is no accord about what the law of nature demands across many cases, individuals consent with each other to negotiate their conflicts through processes they impose on themselves to pacify these disputes. Independent legislative assemblies provide the principal institutional loci where rival interpretations of the common good are sorted out and resolved: "For the People having reserved to themselves the Choice of their Representatives, as the Fence to their Properties, could do it for no other end, but that they might always be freely chosen, and so chosen, freely act and advise, as the necessity of the Commonwealth, and the publick Good should, upon examination, and mature debate, be judged to require" (2.222; see also 2.215). Locke is under no illusions, however, that assemblies will refrain from enacting contentious legislation. Only their right to engage in political activities will encourage people to accept defeat without resorting to violence. A political defeat, unlike a defeat through force, preserves the opportunity for all sides to revisit and renegotiate their choices (2.142–43, 2.153–54, 2.216, 2.222). The specific terms of cooperation they manage to arrive at will be at best a modus vivendi among them; they will have to find ways to muddle through, to work out "a peaceable decision of all their Controversies" (2.227), often choosing among lesser evils, as Locke writes, "as far as is possible" (2.88).

In sum, our reading of the Lockean approach to domestic conflict yields the following principle **(P1): the practices of politics provide the main way of containing discord over rival terms of cooperation short of the recourse to force.**

---

[32] In *Federalist* 1: 4–5, Hamilton similarly argues that "so numerous ... and so powerful are the causes, which serve to give a false bias to the judgement, that we ... see wise and good men on the wrong as well as on the right side of questions, of the first magnitude to society. This circumstance ... would furnish a lesson of moderation to those, who are ever so much persuaded of their being in the right, in any controversy."

[33] In the Table of Contents with summaries of sections of chapters added after the first edition of Locke's *Essay* (1975 [1689]) was published, Book IV, Chapter 16, Section 4 was titled "the right use of it [judgement] is mutual Charity and Forbearance."

Locke's understanding of political life, however, goes beyond the notion that it promises to contain dissensus short of violence. Politics successfully replaces the appeal to force only when it is inclusive, that is, only when every individual has a say in the resolution of their conflicts. Locke begins with a normative claim: because human beings are, "by Nature, all free, equal and independent," there is one, and only one, "way whereby any one devests himself of his Natural Liberty, and puts on the bonds of Civil Society," and that is "by agreeing with other Men to joyn and unite into a Community, for their comfortable, safe, and peaceable living one amongst another, . . . and a greater Security against any that are not of it" (2.95). In other words, membership in the political community is predicated on every individual's express consent (2.122). But, for Locke, this normative demand is only the beginning of politics.[34] He contends that grounding the state's legitimacy on universal consent is the only option that will make sense to individuals subjected to its coercive authority. Their central challenge is to overcome the state of nature's anarchy without embracing tyranny. On the one hand, every individual must agree to abandon the use or the threat to use force for politics to begin; and they will be persuaded to turn to the political resolution of their conflicts only if their disparate interests are acknowledged. To require their consent to terms of cooperation they have no role in negotiating – that is, to exclude anyone from the political process – is in Locke's view both irrational and divorced from reality: "no rational Creature," he writes, "can be supposed to change his condition with an intention to be worse" (2.131; also 2.91, 2.163, 2.164, 2.230). Exclusion from politics is tantamount to tyranny – in Locke's words, the use of "Force without Right" (2.19, 2.232) – and human beings are too contentious and too wedded to their diverse convictions to passively submit to "illegal force" (2.209). On the other, Locke favors representative assemblies elected by a broadly democratic franchise, otherwise the people's fundamental property rights, including the right to their own persons, will not be formally recognized or protected (2.142). Moreover, only if all individuals are broadly included in the political process, especially through their enfranchisement, can they succeed in finding some common ground, by ensuring that their representatives, in enacting legislation, "have weighed the Reasons on all sides" (2.222; also 2.142).[35]

---

[34] That consent is the beginning of politics of course means that the form of government adopted will vary with circumstances, predicated on a particular people's experiences and prudential considerations (see 2.107, 2.111–12, 2.132). Locke rules out only one form of government – absolutism, both because it is inconsistent with natural right and because, as we argue below, it simply makes no sense (2.90–94).

[35] The claim that Locke endorsed a democratic franchise is controversial. The "Second Treatise" is ambiguous, but the weight of the text suggests that Locke favored representative assemblies elected by an extensive franchise, drawing on the lessons of well-framed states, although he left

Political inclusivity played an especially important role in classical liberalism's approach to the challenge of taming conflicts in civil society. Montesquieu
and Madison acknowledged that political liberty exacerbated social dissensus:
"all the passions being unrestrained," wrote Montesquieu (1949 [1748]:
XIX.27.308), "hatred, envy, jealousy, and an ambitious desire of riches and
honors, appear in their extent." Moreover, individuals commonly pursue their
shared interests by forming groups, which only increased their capacity to harm
others and the common good (*Federalist* 10, 1961 [1788]: 56–60). Inclusivity
provided its own solution. As Madison famously argued in *Federalist* 10 (1961
[1788]: 64), the remedy to the social tensions caused by factions was to "extend
the sphere, and you take in a greater variety of parties and interests; you make it
less probable that a majority of the whole will have a common motive to invade
the rights of other citizens; or if such a common motive exists, it will be more
difficult for all who feel it to discover their own strength, and to act in unison
with each other." Political liberty, in sum, fosters a system of checks and
balances by creating a civil society of groups, forcing them to negotiate their
differences precisely because each is rendered impotent against its rivals
(Montesquieu, 1949 [1748]: XIX.27.307–15).[36]

Thus, P1 carries an important corollary **(C1): politics must be inclusive,
broadly representative of all interests, to secure cooperation without
violence.**

Power

Locke's theory of government's creation presupposes a political community
that lasts long enough to exercise its constituent power. In a realist vein, he
maintains that only the concentration of power in the hands of the state can put
an effective end to the anarchy of the state of nature (2.20–21, 2.87–89, 2.124–
127, 2.136, 2.171, 2.212).[37] To be sure, he argues that individuals will consent

---

the actual extent of the franchise to the prudential consideration of people themselves (2.140–43,
2.153–54, 2.157, 2.159, 2.213, 2.222). For a defense of Locke's democratic commitments, see
Ashcraft (1992); for an alternative view, see Wood (1992).

[36] In his *Letter Concerning Toleration*, Locke anticipates this remedy in his response to the fear that
toleration would only abet religious conflicts. To the contrary, he argues, a policy of toleration
would pacify conflict by multiplying the number of religious congregations. Aware that they
have limited power to impose their will on others, he writes (2003 [1689]: 248), "all the several
separate congregations, like so many guardians of the public peace, will watch one another, that
nothing may be innovated or changed in the form of government: because they can hope for
nothing better than what they already enjoy; that is, an equal condition with their fellow-subjects,
under a just and moderate government" (see also pp. 246–47).

[37] Locke's text is ambiguous: some passages of the "Second Treatise" indicate that it is their initial
political association, and not the establishment of the state, that brings a group of individuals out
of the state of nature (2.96–99, 2.211). This ambiguity underscores Locke's assessment of the

to be coerced, that is, to cede to the state their natural power to protect themselves, only "with this express or tacit Trust, That it shall be imployed for their good, and the preservation of their Property" (2.171). Nevertheless, he insists that they must resign to the government the effective exercise of *all* power to make binding decisions for the commonwealth (see Grant, 1987: 78):

> But forasmuch as men thus entering into societies, grounded upon their mutual compacts of assistance, for the defence of their temporal goods, may neverthe-less be deprived of them, either by the rapine and fraud of their fellow-citizens, or by the hostile violence of foreigners: the remedy of this evil consists in arms, riches, and multitudes of citizens: the remedy of others in laws: and the care of all things relating both to the one and the other is committed by the society to the civil magistrate. (Locke, 2003 [1689]: 242)

Locke conceives of government as an "umpire," his apt metaphor for an artificial institutional arrangement intended to adjudicate "all the differences that may happen between any Members of that Society, concerning any matter of right" (2.87). A third party is needed to which disputes may be brought, and those disputes will be resolved inside civil society, not by asking the umpire to judge by natural law, but rather according to institutions and procedures "received and allowed by common consent" (2.124). And the umpire's decision is necessarily final, supplanting "all private judgement of every particular Member" (2.87; also 2.88). No individual may, "by his own Authority, avoid the force of the Law .... No Man in Civil Society can be exempted from the Laws of it" (2.94). "[O]r else this original Compact, whereby he with others incorporates into one Society, would signifie nothing, and be no Compact" (2.97; also 2.96).

The exercise of state power is an ineliminable political problem. There is no shared moral perspective or standpoint, prior to its deployment, which can command any political community's general endorsement. Locke's remedy to the disorder of the state of nature parallels Hobbes's: only a government with supreme power to frame and carry out its decisions can establish specific terms of cooperation. He appeals to historical evidence to show that absolute mon-archies frustrate economic development (1.33). Nevertheless, a community's cooperative enterprises will flourish only under the state's energetic direction (2.42; see Grant, 1987: 111–14). Locke feared the government's arbitrary exercise of power, not its use to organize and protect the commonwealth.

Classical liberals endorsed Hobbes's remedy to the problem of collective action – to create a final authority with sufficient power to make binding

---

tenuousness of the political consensus that begins their transition to civil society. For a discussion of the interpretive difficulties, see Ashcraft (1987: 115–16); Grant (1987: 105–08).

decisions for the whole community. Like Hobbes and Locke, Kant argued that only a state, possessing the supreme coercive power to enforce its judgements, can ensure domestic peace and security from external threats (1991 [1784]: 46, [1792]: 73, 75, 79–82, [1795]: 117, [1797]: 137–38, 142–45; Waldron, 2006: 192–94). Similarly, the aim of the authors of *The Federalist* was to justify the creation of an "energetic" national state (*Federalist* 1: 7; Epstein, 1984: 54). In Hamilton's view, this meant conferring on the national government vast new powers of the purse and sword: "that there ought to be no limitation of a power destined to effect a purpose, which is itself incapable of limitation" (*Federalist* 31, 1961 [1788]: 194; also *Federalist* 1: 6–7, *Federalist* 15: 95–96, *Federalist* 23: 147–48, *Federalist* 30: 190; Epstein, 1984: 35–36).

A Lockean approach to the challenge of collective action thus yields a second principle **(P2): cooperation requires centralized power.** Locke and the classical liberals applied this principle to the domestic realm: only a state with the power to enforce its decisions can ensure coordination among the activities of large numbers of people or groups of people. And, as we will show, such power concentration both requires and reinforces power disparities. We suggest that a similar concentration of power is necessary in the international realm to allow for political (peaceful) processes to unfold.

Unlike Hobbes and like Locke, of course, Montesquieu, Kant, and the authors of *The Federalist* were also liberals, committed to the security of individuals' liberty, from each other and from the state (*Federalist* 10, 1961 [1788]: 57; Kant, 1991 [1797]: 133; Montesquieu, 1949 [1748]: XI.4.150, XI.6.151, XII.2.183–84). Their challenge, as Madison phrased it, "in framing a government which is to be administered by men over men, . . . [is] this: You must first enable the government to controul the governed; and in the next place, oblige it to controul itself" (*Federalist* 51, 1961 [1788]: 349. See also Kant, 1991 [1797]: 134; Montesquieu, 1949 [1748]: XI.4–6.150–51).

Restraining Power

Hobbes (1994 [1651]: XVII.13) famously argued that by the Leviathan's "authority, given him by every particular man in the commonwealth, he hath the use of so much power and strength conferred on him that by terror thereof he is enabled to conform the wills of them all to peace at home and mutual aid against their enemies abroad." Locke's alternative, and that of the classical liberals, is to construct a "*liberalism* of fear," predicated on a *summum malum* that all human beings know and must avoid if they can.[38] While acknowledging Hobbes's premise that human beings are apt to pursue their advantage at others'

---

[38] Shklar (1989: 27; emphasis added). See also Cox (1960: 187); Grant (1987: 203).

expense, Locke maintains that, behind the ceremony of their offices, rulers too are but ordinary human beings, subject to the same self-interested desires. Because government is an instrument to pacify conflicts, and the absolute ruler, in the circumstance of a dispute with any of his subjects, is judge in his own case, his rule institutionalizes partiality, and his subjects "put themselves into a worse condition than the state of Nature" (2.137). Locke appeals to their bitter experience of abuse by their monarch to warn contemporaries that concentrating unchecked power in a ruler's hands simply made no sense. Life in the state of nature, he repeatedly reminds them, cannot long be "endured" (2.13). To remedy its "Inconveniences, ... which must certainly be Great" (2.13), by creating an absolute government, however, "is to think that Men are so foolish that they take care to avoid what Mischiefs may be done them by Pole-Cats, or Foxes, but are content, nay think it Safety, to be devoured by Lions" (2.93; also 2.137). He draws his contemporaries' attention to an indispensable task: because governments are necessarily charged with "the care of all things relating" to legislation and enforcement, and the active encouragement of "arms, riches, and multitudes of citizens" (Locke, 2003 [1689]: 242), there will always be a need to restrain their power and to protect the independence of individuals and groups outside the state.

Locke's account of the formation of states, reaching "back as far as Records give us any account of Peopling the World" (2.106), traces their origin to the patriarchal family, "having accustomed [its members] to the Rule of one Man" (2.107; also 2.105–112). The original patriarchs, in his view, "though they command absolutely in War, yet at home and in time of Peace ... exercise very little Dominion, and have but a very moderate Sovereignty," so that even "the Resolutions of Peace and War" were normally retained by "the People," or exercised "in a Council" (2.108). The extension of political authority to adjudicate internal disputes – for example, "the itinerant justices sent out from the King's court from 1166 onwards" (Tully, 1993: 136) – was a later development. People tacitly acquiesced to this original "petty" monarchy. The need for power concentration within the state originally implied acknowledging power disparities and accepting some advantages for the powerful. The original patriarchs, however, had little reason to abuse their power because material scarcity "afforded little matter for Covetousness or Ambition" (2.107), and "gave Men no Temptation to enlarge their Possessions of Land, or contest for wider extent of Ground" (2.108). And the people had little to fear from their rule, "which from their Infancy they had been all accustomed to; and which, by experience they had found both easie and safe" (2.107). Early modern economic growth and political centralization overturned these conditions: "Ambition and Luxury ... taught Princes to have distinct and separate Interests from their

People," and stretch their "Prerogative . . . to oppress" them, so that "Men found it necessary to examine more carefully the Original and Rights of Government," and introduce formal means of restraining its power (2.111; also 2.107).

Locke's historical sketch is his answer to Robert Filmer's defense of patriarchy, justifying unconditional obedience to the Stuart monarchy. It is also intended to frame his solution to the political conflicts attending the consolidation of royal absolutism in the seventeenth century (Tully, 1993: 36–37). Locke likely had in mind a constituent assembly responsible for authorizing a majority of its members, or "any number greater than the majority," to reconsider the government's institutional design (2.99; also 2.242–43; Tully, 1993: 12, 40). Unanimity of all the members is not only unobtainable (2.98); it is not, as Grant points out (1987: 118), "a properly political principle. Where unanimous consent is required to reach a decision, each individual actually continues to be governed by his own judgement."

The majority's challenge is twofold. First, it must undertake to design a system of formidable institutional mechanisms that cabin the government's arbitrary exercise of coercion: to "restrain" or "limit" it, to place "fences" and "guards" around the use of power, ensuring the "safety," "protection," and "security" of the people (2.17, 2.87, 2.93–94, 2.107, 2.111, 2.136–138, 2.149, 2.222, 2.227). Second, Locke acknowledges that institutional checks are liable to fail (2.201). Discord, however, will attend any one individual's or group's judgement that government has overreached. A prudent majority must therefore establish mechanisms of accountability that provide the people with "manifest evidence" that their government has transgressed its constitutional boundaries (2.230; also 2.213).

Locke allows political communities a wide degree of discretion in fashioning their form of government "as they think good" according to their history, convenience, and prudence (2.132; also 2.135, 2.138, 2.142, 2.153–54, 2.156–57, 2.213). Nevertheless, he encourages his contemporaries to think in specific and concrete terms about the form of government they create. Locke makes explicit constitutional recommendations drawing on the lessons of "well order'd Commonwealths" (2.143). Underlying these recommendations are prudential judgments assessing alterative institutional mechanisms of constraining the power of the state.

Locke of course established classical liberalism's special focus on a system of checks and balances. Classical liberals endorsed a variety of mechanisms to curb the government's coercive power, including the rule of law, the constitutional separation of powers, and federalism.[39] Locke offered two such

---

[39] Scholars focusing on the work of classical liberals rightly underscore the differences between their institutional prescriptions and Locke's. For example, Ward (2007: 556) points out that, in contrast to Locke, "who confined the separation of powers to the division of the legislative and

mechanisms: the rule of law and the separation of legislative and executive power, both backed in the final analysis by popular vigilance. Legal supremacy forms the organizing principle of limited government: rulers must themselves be ruled by the laws they make (2.93, 2.137).[40] Although rule confers advantages on the powerful, legal supremacy subjects them to two types of constraints. First, laws must apply equally to the powerful and the weak. The legislature is "to govern by promulgated establish'd Laws, not to be varied in particular Cases, but to have one Rule for Rich and Poor, for the Favourite at Court, and the Country Man at Plough" (2.142, also 2.94). Second, legislation must be interpreted and applied to particular cases "by indifferent and upright Judges" (2.131), whose independence is protected from any "manifest perverting of Justice, and a barefaced wresting of the Laws, to protect or indemnifie the violence or injuries of some Men, or Party of Men" (2.20; also 2.94). In the absence of these conditions, rule by law amounts to little more than the brute power of rulers (2.20, 2.94, 2.137, 2.149, 2.199, 2.214, 2.222). Corruption of the impartial administration of justice provides critical evidence that the system of umpirage has broken down, justifying resistance and revolution.

The separation of legislative and executive functions is the second mechanism constraining the state's coercive power. Their experience of absolute government, Locke argues, pressed individuals to "trouble themselves to think of Methods of restraining any Exorbitances of those, to whom they had given Authority over them, and of ballancing the Power of Government, by placing several parts of it in different hands" (2.107). Well-framed polities separate legislative and executive power, "because it may be too great a temptation to humane frailty apt to grasp at Power, for the same Persons who have the Power of making Laws, to have also in their hands the power to execute them, whereby they may exempt themselves from Obedience to the Laws they make, and suit the Law, both in its making and execution, to their own private advantage" (2.143; also 2.152, 2.159).

The community's "first and fundamental positive Law . . . is the establishing of the Legislative Power . . . . This Legislative is not only the supream power of the Common-wealth, but sacred and unalterable in the hands where the Community have once placed it" (2.134; also 2.212). The reason for the

---

executive, Montesquieu highlights the additional significance of the independent English judiciary as a protection for due process" (see also Shklar, 1987: 88, Manent 1995: 56–58). Without minimizing these differences, we maintain that these institutional innovations are alternative means of achieving the same goal: to organize the state's structure so as "to preserve [its] necessary energy while discouraging its unnecessary use or abuse" (Epstein, 1984: 49).

[40] As commentators have rightly noted, Locke abandoned the concept of sovereignty dominant in 17th century England in favor of the concept of legal supremacy. See Grant (1987: 78); Tully (1993: 37); Ward (2006: 691–705).

legislature's supremacy is not that legislators are superior guardians of natural law, but rather that it is a safer repository than alternatives of the trust that it will serve as a neutral umpire. Independent legislative assemblies, as we've seen, are the principal institutional loci of domestic politics. "For 'tis not a certain number of Men, no, nor their meeting, unless they have also Freedom of debating, and Leisure of perfecting, what is for the good of the Society wherein the Legislative consists" (2.215; also 2.222). Locke repeatedly appeals to the executive's arbitrary interference with the legislature and elections, "or ways of Election," as concrete evidence that it has overreached, undercutting established mechanisms designed to limit it (2.216; also 2.155, 2.168, 2.215, 2.222).

Legislative supremacy is the principal check on executive power, so that the executive "is visibly subordinate and accountable to it" (2.152; see also 2.153). But Locke is also suspicious that the legislature will prove untrustworthy, imprudent, and prone to abuse its power (2.149, 2.222. See Tully, 1993: 37–39). Assemblies themselves must be controlled to avoid the partiality of legislators (2.138). Unchecked popular assemblies, meeting frequently and at length, "without necessary occasion" (2.156), are susceptible to "think themselves to have a distinct interest, from the rest of the Community; and so will be apt to increase their own Riches and Power, by taking, what they think fit, from the People ... though there be good and equitable Laws to set the bounds" of property (2.138, also 2.94, 2.143). He proposes two internal restraints on the legislature's power. First, although assemblies may be "placed in one or more" persons, or "be always in being, or only by intervals" (2.135; also 2.138, 2.142), Locke favors "Governments where the Legislative consists, wholly or in part, in Assemblies which are variable," that is, subject to limited sessions, "whose Members upon the Dissolution of the Assembly, are Subjects under the common Laws of their Country, equally with the rest" (2.138). Second, legislative sessions are delimited by a combination of constitutional prescription and executive prerogative (2.154–158). The executive's power to disallow legislation, and to convene, prorogue, or dissolve assemblies as needed, serves as the principal check on the legislature's tendency to corruption (2.153, 2.167).

The executive's prerogative is equally important (2.159–160, 2.164). General rules cannot anticipate every exigency, legislatures are too numerous and too slow to deal with emergencies, and the application of laws to specific cases may be unjust, requiring executive discretion to mitigate legal punishment or issue pardons (2.159–60). Locke argues that executives have an extensive reach especially in the conduct of foreign policy (2.147). He does not, however, as some scholars suggest, argue that an expansive executive prerogative is necessary to empower enlightened rulers to apply the obligations of natural law (see, e.g., Fatovic, 2004). "Such God-like Princes," Locke writes, "indeed had some

Title to Arbitrary Power." Yet he cautions that, upon this thinking "is founded that saying, That the Reigns of good Princes have been always most dangerous to the Liberties of their People" (2.166; also 2.94). Well-framed states, that is, constitutionally delimit the executive's prerogative power (2.162. See Ward, 2005: 732–38). Nevertheless, relying on constitutional language alone to restrain the executive's legitimate discretion, subject to the "trust always to have it exercised only for the publick Weal" (2.156), will prove inadequate. Much like Madison (Letter to Jefferson, October 1788), Locke was skeptical that "parchment barriers," rather than institutional ones, would confine the abuse of executive power, "for it is not Names, that Constitute Governments, but the use and exercise of those Powers that were intended to accompany them" (2.215; also 2.138, 2.151–52).

Locke remains unconvinced that even institutional checks, on their own, are sufficient to prevent the government from abusing its power. Popular vigilance is necessary to restrain rulers' temptation to override the limitations placed on them. Popular action takes two forms: elections and revolution. Periodic democratic elections play an especially salient role in cabining the legislative and the executive, adjudicating conflicts between them, and in providing the people a redress mechanism short of rebellion to prevent violations of their trust (2.142, 2.154, 2.155, 2.216, 2.222. See Ashcraft, 1987: 213–16). Periodic elections provide a means of protecting people's safety and security: they are not only a way of sorting out popular views but of making it more difficult for rulers to entrench their power (2.134, 2.143, 2.153, 2.222).

Elections themselves, however, may prove insufficient to prevent governments from abusing the trust reposed in them (see 2.242). "'Tis a Mistake," warns Locke, "to think" that the arbitrary use of power "is proper only to Monarchies; other Forms of Government are liable to it, as well as that" (2.201). At this point, the bare agreement to avoid the resolution of conflicts by violence, to mediate differences by the political practices of negotiation and compromise, unravels.[41] All individuals retain an indefeasible right to "appeal to heaven," to turn to revolutionary violence, to protect "themselves from the attempts and designs of any Body, even of their Legislators, whenever they shall be so foolish, or so wicked, as to lay and carry on designs against the Liberties and Properties of the Subject" (2.149; also 2.129–30, 2.155, 2.168, 2.240–243).

---

[41] This was in fact Locke's own political experience in the 1680s. "The *Two Treatises of Government*," writes Ashcraft (1987: 28), "was one of a small handful of revolutionary tracts ... defending the right of subjects to take up arms against the government." For an analysis of the broader contemporary breakdown in the willingness to settle differences by political compromise, see Ashcraft (1986: 128–80).

Locke recognizes that his theory of revolution is "the most controversial and unconventional aspect of the *Two treatises*"; human partiality makes the appeal to revolutionary violence especially troubling (see Tully, 1993: 44).[42] He revisits the question whether the threat to political stability is "oftener" due to the governments' abuse of power or popular disobedience, a question that he leaves to "impartial History to determine" (2.230). Nevertheless, because political power must lie somewhere, Locke thinks it lies more safely in the people's hands (2.91, 2.163, 2.223–24, 2.230–31, 2.239). He is persuaded that human beings have less to fear from the perils of rebellion than the perils of tyranny (2.224–230). In using force without right, government declares war on its subjects. Its decision to rule by violence is nothing short of an attempt to reduce the people to a condition of slavery (2.239). Indeed, because every form of government will abuse its power, Locke concludes that not merely the threat, but the actual practice of popular rebellion is necessary to enforce limits on its arbitrary use (2.149, 2.226, 2.228, 2.240–243). Popular rebellion by the "rabble" is a necessary part of a strategy of damage control, ensuring good government and, paradoxically, political stability (2.209).

The aim of Locke's "liberalism of fear" is to balance the necessary concentration of power with institutional restraints on its use; in his words, to "prevent the Abuses of that Power which [people] having intrusted in another's hands only for their own good, they found was made use of to hurt them" (2.111). A Lockean approach to domestic and international politics therefore yields a third principle **(P3): the need to develop institutional mechanisms to restrain the abuse of power.**

We should underscore that these three principles – the "legs" of the Lockean tripod – are interdependent, each relying on the others to create a liberal order, but also in tension with one another, requiring an ongoing process of balancing and rebalancing among them. Politics presupposes a bare agreement to abandon the use of force in favor of the practices of negotiation and accommodation (P1). It must also broadly include all relevant stakeholders (C1), both so that they can be enticed to abandon the recourse to force, and so that they can work out terms of cooperation acceptable to all. However, the concentration of coercive power (P2)

---

[42] An element of subjectivity remains an ineliminable part of Locke's politics. However much their compact excludes "all private judgement of every particular Member, . . . [and] the Community comes to be Umpire, by settled standing Rules, indifferent, and the same to all Parties" (2.87; also 2.243), it is nevertheless the case that "every Man is Judge for himself" (2.241) whether their government's umpirage has irretrievably broken down, and whether he will join with others to "erect a new Form, or under the old form place it in new hands, as they think good" (2.243). Kant (1991 [1792]: 81) categorically rejected a right to revolution precisely because it allowed private judgements about justice to usurp the judgement of the community. For an argument mitigating Kant's strictures on resistance, see Waldron (2006: 196–97).

or, to use Hamilton's word (Federalist 1: 7), "energetic" government, will be required to implement any solution to their collective action problems. And power concentration inevitably will give some groups an advantage over others. A Lockean approach to resolving our inevitable dissensus, both domestic and international, therefore requires an ongoing balancing between politics, which is generally egalitarian, and the concentration of power, which is hierarchical and reinforces disparities. Institutional restraints on coercive power (P3) offer critical mechanisms to reconcile the tensions between the two other "legs." But restraints, too, need to be balanced with political processes (P1) that shape the institutions checking concentrated power (P3) and the powerful bodies (P2) responsible for framing and enacting public policies. A Lockean approach does not prescribe a specific balance among the three principles. Rather, the balance achieved in any given set of circumstances is itself a product of existing conditions.

3 Applying Lockean (Classical) Liberalism to International Relations

The Domestic-International Analogy: Groups as the Main Political "Actors"

How does one apply the three aforementioned principles derived from Locke's work and complemented by the writings of other classical liberals to the international realm? As discussed, the application of these principles has to be based on an analogy between the domestic and international realms because international conditions at the time Locke and his immediate successors shaped classical liberalism were very different from those we experience today and did not allow them to extend their arguments about politics within the state to specific ones outside the state.

We begin from the understanding that any useful parallel needs to avoid the facile comparison between individuals (in the domestic realm) and states (in the international realm) that has been the focus of the vast majority of such analogies (e.g., Suganami, 2008). Rather, following the classical liberals, we maintain that all politics (at the core of the first Lockean principle), domestic or international, unfolds among groups. In the domestic realm these have variously taken the form of political parties, "factions" within or across such parties, groups of nobles or ecclesiastics in the Middle Ages, ethnic or religious groups, or civil society organizations. These groups sometimes are part of (or "in") government and sometimes not.

The most important groups involved in politics in the international realm are, of course, individual states. However, numerous transnational nongovernmental groups, such as NGOs, multinational corporations, or labor groups, also play critical roles in world politics. More important, states often come together in groups to act in unison and achieve common goals. Groupings of developing countries such as the Non-Aligned Movement or the G-77 have long been seen as consequential actors in world politics. More recently, BRICS countries have formed a particularly significant group seeking to challenge United States and, more broadly, Western global leadership (i.e., that of another group of states).

Finally, the most powerful states in the world have often come together as a group in international institutions, for example, the Concert of Europe or UN Security Council. Sometimes they have had common interests such as stability in Europe or retaining permanent membership and veto power exclusively in their hands, respectively, leading them to act together. Other times they have had very divergent interests and failed to coordinate their actions. However, the same can be said of all groups, whether they are made up of individuals from the same political parties, states, or transnational NGOs. The political science literature, whether focusing on domestic or international developments, has most often analyzed such relatively heterogeneous groups as the main actors in political processes.

It is particularly important to consider groups rather than individual actors in any political analysis, whether domestic or international, because the former are in fact the holders of power (the element at the center of Locke's second principle). This argument has long been accepted and is perhaps best reflected in the words of Arendt (2014: 143), who argued that "power is never the property of an individual; it belongs to a group and remains in existence only so long as the group keeps together." Consequently, restraints on power, underlying P3, also have to be thought of as applying to groups.

This focus on groups, rather than single actors, allows us to challenge the notion that power may be concentrated solely in one locus, whether an absolute government in the domestic realm (the "sovereign," according to Bodin, or the "Leviathan," according to Hobbes) or a hegemonic state in the international realm, one that, as far back as Thucydides, has been understood as having virtually complete control over other states (Worth, 2015). Nor can the Hobbesian model of a single center of power refer to an increasingly powerful IGO, or even to a potential forthcoming global government (something that even realists consider; see, e.g., Morgenthau 1993, chapter 29, titled "The World State"). Rather, as we will show, because politics takes place among groups, power is virtually always distributed among *multiple* centers, both in the domestic and international spheres.

The domestic-international analogy we present here is thus between the *various loci of concentrated power* in both realms. Indeed, the dominant existing approach to domestic-international analogies is built on the false assumption that power concentration is dichotomous. Either it exists (and is embodied in an individual or in a state or global institution) or it does not exist. Like most useful concepts in the social sciences, we see power concentration as a question of degree, on a continuum. This assumption allows us to move away from the ubiquitous individual-state analogy between domestic and international politics. Locke's work, differentiating between lions (where more power is concentrated) and polecats and foxes (other, less significant, loci of power concentration) embraces such an approach. His arguments that not only the executive, but the legislative power, needs to be restrained, similarly describes political systems with *multiple* centers of power, albeit instilling different degrees of fear in their respective power. By acknowledging that power is usually spread out across multiple centers in both realms, that it may vary between instances when there is a greater degree of concentration in one locus or a more equal concentration across multiple loci, and that every center of power may instill *some* fear, we can indeed apply the Lockean domestic arguments to the international one.

As the above examples suggest, many international groups have interacted in IGOs, the main stage where international politics currently take place. IGOs can thus be understood as institutions that open up the necessary space for political processes, similar to the national assemblies and parliaments that have existed in the domestic realm for many centuries, offering the principal alternative to resolving international dissensus through the use of force. Based on such an understanding of international politics, it appears that the first Lockean principle, derived in our second section, has indeed been applied in many instances to the international realm. In the following section, we will follow the evolution of the application of this principle (P1) and of the corollary that derives from it (C1) to international relations.

Secondly, the understanding of domestic and international groups as the main political actors allows us to compare the extent to which P2, which states that the concentration of power is necessary to underwrite cooperation, has been applied to domestic and international politics. Our analogy, however, takes into account the different degrees of power concentration in states and IGOs and the multiple centers of such concentration at various times.

The classical liberals wrote in response to the consolidation of power in early modern European states as effective units of government. However, this outcome was the result of a long historical process. Starting with the original patriarchs discussed by Locke, in the Middle Ages sovereignty was divided among multiple groups, which acted as a break on the centralizing power of the monarchy. Kings often vied for power with local nobles, ecclesiastics, and urban centers, which could enact and apply laws across "their" territory. For example, in France, it was only in the twelfth century that the king (Louis VI) began issuing ordinances that applied to the entire territory over which he ruled. Up to that point there was only local, but little to no national taxation (Shennan, 1968: 10). The state as a whole was relatively weak, concentrating only *some* of the power in the system (around the king), while other groups also exercised jurisdiction within their particular domains. The emergence of centralized European states in the seventeenth and eighteenth centuries represented a consolidation of power, as monarchs brought under their sway many of the groups that had previously vied to be more independent. In Louis XIV's case, for example, this consolidation was accompanied by the symbolic physical move of the aristocracy for extended periods of time to the king's newly established court in Versailles. Power consolidation also led to decision-making advantages for the dominant groups that came together to form "the state," reinforcing existing power disparities or creating new ones. The writings of classical liberals such as Locke and Montesquieu were the result of the growing fear of the main center of concentrated power ("the lion") and, consequently, their search for ways to restrain it.

We posit that the current global governance system is undergoing similar processes of power concentration analogous to domestic ones toward the end of the Middle Ages and *before* the processes of state consolidation. In both instances, there are multiple centers of power. In the international realm, the main loci of power concentration are still a handful of four to five dominant states. However, just as in the late Middle Ages, when the central state emerged and came to be recognized as an increasingly important locus of power concentration, we suggest that some IGOs are slowly emerging as additional centers of power concentration, joining the traditional ones represented by dominant states (Grigorescu, 2023).

Clearly, IGOs are not equivalent to Hobbes's Leviathan with a *monopoly* over coercive force. Nevertheless, some of them constitute formidable centers of power concentration, alongside those of dominant states. In some cases, other groups, especially small developing states, fear the concentrated power in such IGOs, as the World Bank or IMF, even more than they fear the United States or China. Decisions of such global institutions may have a greater impact on and erode the sovereignty of small states more than the actions of the most powerful states. Similarly, when East European states sought membership in European institutions in the early 1990s, the conditions put in place by the EU imposed restrictions on these countries that some considered comparable to those that the Soviet Union had applied, especially in that regional hegemon's last years of existence (Lane, 2007: 463). The fear of power concentration in IGOs is especially relevant if one considers the economic realm, not just the security realm.

IGOs became more influential in the 1990s. This influence was reflected both in the increasing number of tasks they took on and in their intrusiveness. The immediate post–Cold War era saw the establishment of the consequential World Trade Organization. The International Criminal Court also emerged around that time and filled an important gap in global governance, allowing for a permanent court to reach legal decisions against individuals (rather than states) for genocide, war crimes, crimes against humanity, and crimes of aggression. The transformation of the European Communities into the European Union in 1992 broadened the organization's influence over additional issues, including the very intrusive ones of monetary policy (through a new European Bank) and foreign and security policy. Many of these organizations, as well as some existing ones, came to usurp a good deal of decision-making power from states. All states, but especially smaller ones, thus came to fear IGOs' increased potential influence as a threat to their sovereignty. These developments led observers to seek restraints on (and accountability of) international institutions, just as classical liberalism sought restraints on increasingly powerful national institutions centuries earlier (P3).

The main reason for the increased role of IGOs was, as mentioned earlier, the greater agreement between the United States and Russia, the two powerful adversaries of the Cold War. China, at that time, was also more likely to agree with the other great powers. In sum, it was the relative consensus among these states that individually represented the centers of greatest power aggregation up to that time, and their coming together in groups, that led to even greater concentrated power than before. Such power concentration took place, for example, through the collusion of the permanent members of the UNSC, or among the now virtually unopposed "Western" states in the IMF, World Bank, and even NATO.

This collusion enabled the UNSC to approve more peacekeeping operations. The same general agreement between great powers and the lack of other credible alternative power centers gave the Bretton Woods institutions increased influence in the 1990s and early 2000s. In sum, a first reason that IGOs became more influential was that power *could* now be concentrated to back them up.

A second reason that IGOs became more powerful was the greater *need* for them to solve collective action problems (P2). Indeed, the turn of the twenty-first century witnessed a growing number of global challenges that could best be resolved multilaterally rather than unilaterally. The economic, social, health, environmental, or security effects of globalization required powerful international institutions to deal with them (Keohane, 2001: 2–3). This process is analogous to the one that led to more powerful domestic institutions in the late

Middle Ages, when national security or economic concerns led to stronger roles for national governments (e.g., Strayer, 2005).

The process whereby IGOs assumed an increased role also required greater expertise (and, consequently, empowerment) of these organizations' bureaucracies. Even states that were not strong supporters of IGO secretariats' autonomy often acquiesced to it as an inevitable byproduct of their increased specialization necessary for more effective governance (also related to P2). This process also paralleled domestic developments whereby civil servants became more specialized and autonomous, starting in the nineteenth century when governments began introducing meritocratic systems, replacing the predominance of patronage (Rouban, 2007).[43]

From the UN's Oil for Food Program, in Iraq, to the IMF's response to the Asian Financial Crisis, experts, representatives of states, and the general public often blamed IGO officials rather than powerful member-states for their organizations' mistakes. These examples suggested to many that IGO secretariats had become more autonomous from the member-states (e.g., Barnett and Finnemore, 2004; Hawkins et al., 2006; Oestreich, 2012), and thus contributed even further to the view that IGOs formed centers for power concentration, having an impact on the lives of billions of people, that is, they came to *matter* (e.g., Keohane, 2001: 7). This argument was especially present in the broad literature on the EU (e.g., Curtin, 1999).

All such developments, leading to perceptions that IGOs were becoming more powerful, triggered in turn increased calls to develop institutional restraints not just on the power of the dominant states, but also on those of IGOs. In sum, in the international realm, the application of P2 and P3 requires us to consider the importance both of the power of dominant states *and* the power of IGOs. Sometimes such states support IGO initiatives and sometimes they do not, in a similar fashion as various powerful domestic groups in medieval times supported or opposed the state led by the king.

Overall, this more complex domestic–international analogy, focusing on groups and multiple centers of power concentration, allows us to draw the necessary parallels between the degree to which the three Lockean principles have been applied to the international realm. The following three sections will offer narratives of (1) the evolution of IGOs as loci for political interactions (P1), especially for inclusive interactions (C1); (2) the increasing role of IGOs and their emergence as additional centers of power concentration (besides the ones represented by dominant states) in order to achieve common goals (P2); (3) the efforts to restrain the concentrated power of both dominant states and IGOs

---

[43] In China meritocratic bureaucratic systems were introduced about two thousand years earlier.

(P3). We also note why there have been problems implementing the principles in the international realm and show which groups supported and opposed them.

The First Lockean Principle and Corollary as Applied to the International Realm

(P1): the practices of politics provide the main way of containing discord over rival terms of cooperation short of the recourse to force.

(C1): politics must be inclusive, broadly representative of all interests, to secure cooperation without violence.

P1, of course, runs counter to the IR realist view that embraced Clausewitz's understanding that war is "simply the continuation of political intercourse with the addition of other means" (von Clausewitz, 1918: 24). Instead, it is similar to the neoliberal institutionalist perspective emphasizing the need for bargaining (as opposed to the interwar IR liberal focus on identifying already existing common interests) as a way to alter interests in the search for common ground and to avoid the use of force.

Indeed, international institutions can be understood as the embodiment of P1 as they establish a forum for political processes. They are the main loci of contestation in global governance (Zürn, 2018). Starting with the Concert of Europe, states have come together in such institutions to seek peaceful ways of resolving their differences to avoid use of force. Although the Concert (generally considered an informal institution) and the river commissions of the early nineteenth century (the first formal IGOs) were fairly exclusive, bringing together only the most powerful states or riparian states, respectively, by the second half of the nineteenth century IGOs such as the International Telegraph Union (ITU), Universal Postal Union, or Permanent Court of Arbitration (PCA), began allowing for virtually universal state membership, thus indicating that inclusivity of participation (C1) had come to be increasingly accepted in the international realm.

Inclusivity was not won, however, without conflict between the most important international groups of actors. The clashes over inclusivity especially unfolded at the establishment of the all-important League of Nations, in 1919. The original plans for the League (drawn up by representatives of the United States and United Kingdom) called for an IGO with a powerful Council meeting permanently and a very weak Assembly that would only meet every few years (similar to the practice in the ITU). In those plans, only the five most powerful states were to be represented in the Council. Moreover, whereas the Council was intended to discuss all matters, the Assembly was originally envisaged to deal only with issues that were not part of the Council's purview, which implied that this larger forum would not take on security topics. Small states "revolted" when seeing these first plans for the League and eventually were able to have (1) four of their representatives (by rotation) included in the Council and (2) the rules allow for the Assembly to take up all issues in its debates, including those referring to security (Miller, 1928: 84).

In the end, the question of the League of Nations' inclusivity appeared more problematic when it came to the powerful states than to small ones. The lack of incentives for great powers to be members of the IGO led some to refuse joining (in the case of United States) or to leave (in the case of Germany, Italy, Japan, and USSR). This lack of representation of all states' interests in the League has been cited among the reasons for its failure and even for the outbreak of World War II, an argument in accord with C1. In part, because of the League's inability to act as a locus for politics, the UN founders went to great lengths to encourage powerful states to use the IGO as a place for ongoing bargaining, even in the 1950s, when the two main groups (formed around the two poles of power: the United States and USSR) had few other interactions with each other.

Since the emergence of the League and UN, numerous other IGOs have allowed virtually all states to come together and shape common policies, most of them dealing with issues outside of the security realm. Indeed, one of the lessons that came out of World War II was that the heightened tensions between states could derive from domestic economic and social concerns, not only from direct security crises. The inclusion of the ECOSOC (formally on par with the UNSC) in the UN, as well as the emergence of the World Bank and IMF in the immediate post–World War II era, reflect the trend of states seeking multiple institutions for peaceful *political* interactions to resolve their differences. In sum, IGOs have evolved over more than a century in ways that allow for the application of P1 (and, to a great extent, of C1) to the international realm, just as national institutions have long allowed domestic groups to come together in political processes.

While the prescriptions deriving from C1 appear to have already been accepted through the broadening of IGO membership to virtually all states, the inclusivity of such organizations has considerable room for improvement. After all, states are not the only types of groups that can aggregate individuals' interests in the international realm. To return to the domestic-international analogy, we are reminded that truly inclusive domestic political processes involve not only political parties but other groupings (or, to use Madison's language, "factions"). Similarly, in the international realm, inclusive forums that allow for the representation of cross-cutting interests need to allow for a voice for transnational NGOs, transnational labor groups, ethnic minorities, or even transnational business groups. In this regard, we have also seen important advances in the inclusivity of international political processes. Many IGOs have established bodies allowing for non-state forms of representation such as the organs in the International Labor Organization that included representatives of labor groups and employers or the World Health Organization's Framework for Engagement with Non-State Actors.

Moreover, almost all IGOs have slowly begun to open up and include representatives of international NGOs in their consultations. While this process experienced significant developments even in the interwar era, it has become much more visible in recent decades (e.g., Scholte, 2011; Steffek and Nanz, 2008). The degree to which NGOs have been allowed to play relevant roles in international politics has varied across time and organizations. The literature has noted that developing countries have generally been more likely to oppose the involvement of such global civil society organizations in IGOs' work than developed ones (Grigorescu, 2015; Tallberg et al., 2013).

Thus, overall, although IGOs have emerged as important fora for the unfolding of international politics (P1) and have become fairly inclusive in terms of the *states* that are part of deliberations, they can be even more inclusive of the broad global *interests* represented in their discussions (C1). Such additional interests may be best represented by nongovernmental actors analogous to the civil society that has developed in the domestic realm of liberal polities.

The Second Lockean Principle as Applied to the International Realm

(P2): cooperation requires centralized power.

The second Lockean principle also translates well to the international realm. While it was originally promoted by the Hobbesian liberals of the interwar era, it was not truly applied to the League. This flaw in the IGO's design was due to the decision to downplay the importance of power disparities among states which, inevitably, led powerful states to not join or leave the organization and, inevitably, to its lack of the necessary power concentration to back collective decisions, as suggested earlier. The failure of the League was a hard lesson that led all international institutions established since World War II to give important roles to the dominant states. A new understanding took hold that their power was necessary for backing the organizations' tasks. Their importance to the governance of IGOs has been institutionalized both through formal and informal rules (e.g., Stone, 2011). Indeed, the UN gave the five dominant states formal or de facto permanent representation in its major organs: UNSC, ECOSOC, and

Trusteeship Council. Additionally, they have at least one of their nationals sitting on the ICJ since the inception of the UN. Moreover, early on, more than two thirds of the staff in the UN Secretariat came from these five states. Great powers were also given larger shares of votes in the IMF and World Bank. Of course, these developments, deriving from P2, are in tension with P1, requiring, as noted earlier, a delicate balance between these essential Lockean principles. The continuously changing balance (and tension) between relative equality in participation in deliberations by all states and unequal roles in decision-making has long been discussed in IR literature (e.g., Viola et al., 2015).

P2 has also been increasingly applied in terms of the empowerment of IGOs themselves, not just of the dominant member-states. As mentioned, such organizations are more involved in global policymaking than the international institutions established a century or even half a century earlier. A reflection of the increased influence of IGOs are the many public protests against such organizations, rather than against the powerful states backing them. Some of the first protests unfolded in the late 1980s when global activists condemned several of the World Bank's decisions, most famously the one involving the Sardar Sarovar Dam project in India. Their main concern was with the Bank's staff and its secretive decision-making process, even more than with the government of India or of the major powers that control decision-making in the organization (Udall, 1998). In fact, such criticism led member-states to alter the rules guiding the Bank's public access to information policy. The violent 1999 Seattle demonstrations against the WTO also focused more on the IGO, its flawed practices, and extraordinary (aggregate) power, than on individual dominant members (e.g., Page, 1999). The press reflected the growing power of IGOs, for example, criticizing the UN as an institution, rather than its member-states or the five permanent members of the UNSC, for its poor administration of the Oil-for-Food Program in Iraq (e.g., Gordon, 2006).

As mentioned, the greater concentration of power in IGOs is primarily due to the need for resolving an increasing number of global governance issues and to the intermittent agreements between great powers on such common solutions. The demand for effective organizations has sometimes led to a purposeful promotion of IGO staff autonomy that began with the League of Nations. Other times, however, such autonomy continued to develop even when member-states at least partially opposed it.

The League's first Secretary General, Eric Drummond, deliberately chose a model for the Secretariat making its staff formally autonomous from member-states, rather than under the control of the governments that directly appointed such officials (as had been the case on previous IGOs) (Dubin, 1983: 472). In time, powerful states have generally been the most vocal opponents of such autonomy. This was most evident in times of great global tensions, as in the 1930s, when Germany and Italy sought to control their nationals in the League Secretariat, or in the 1950s, when the USSR and United States sought to adopt rules eroding staff autonomy in the UN (as well as in many of its specialized agencies, such as UNESCO and the ILO).

Yet, despite such efforts from powerful states, the secretariats have become increasingly autonomous, acquiring greater influence in international affairs. Their growing autonomy has been in part the result of a slow process that allowed for the development of various institutions in IGOs such as staff unions, impartial administrative tribunals, or whistleblower policies. In debates surrounding these developments, small states generally supported staff autonomy. This has been especially true starting in the second half of the Cold War, as IGOs included more nationals from developing countries in their secretariats. As small states increasingly saw IGO bureaucracies as potentially siding with them, they backed the aforementioned institutions while dominant states often opposed them (Martinetti, 2006).

Another illustration of the increased separate power of international institutions can be found in the evolution of international courts that have become increasingly independent of members-states. As they did, states found it in their interests to take their cases to these institutions for adjudication, in a similar way that increasingly independent domestic courts came to be used by more domestic actors starting in the early fourteenth century (e.g., Shennan, 1968: 10). This process has, in turn, led to more active international courts over the past century.

In sum, P2 appears to have been increasingly applied to the international realm, both in terms of a greater role for powerful states in IGOs and of greater influence of the IGOs themselves. Due to small states' opposition, dominant states have not gained an even greater control over IGOs. Conversely, due to great power opposition, IGOs themselves have not become as independent and powerful as P2 entails. Overall, although the trend has been toward growing concentration, it has waxed and waned across time. Most importantly, power concentration in IGOs has slowed down in the twenty-first century as the dominant states moved toward more discordant positions.

To further advance our ability to deal with the many global tasks we face, a Lockean approach to IR suggests that international institutions should become even more powerful. For that to happen, both powerful states and weaker ones should tame their respective opposition to institutional changes and seek additional "constitutional bargains" that consider both power disparities and broad participation, such as those that were struck after major wars or even after the Cold War (Ikenberry, 2001). With the advent of nuclear weapons, states need to accept such bargains without waiting for major wars to shake up global power structures.

The Third Lockean Principle as Applied to the International Realm

(P3): the need to develop institutional mechanisms to restrain the abuse of power.

The evolution of international relations also suggests that the third principle derived from Locke's work has been increasingly applied to the international realm. When discussing P2, we considered both concentrated power in the hands of individual dominant states and the concentrated power in IGOs which, in turn, referred to the aggregate power of the dominant states and, to some degree the growing power of IGO secretariats. Similarly, we consider both the institutions that restrain powerful states and those that restrain IGOs.

Continuing our parallel to classical liberal approaches to domestic institutions, we examine whether and how IGO assemblies (analogous to domestic national assemblies) and international courts (analogous to domestic courts) have evolved to keep concentrated power in check. These two types of institutions are, after all, the main ones discussed by Locke and classical liberals as restraining the concentrated power of the executive.

IGO assemblies have been discussed above as primarily relevant for P1, as they offer the necessary space for inclusive political processes. However, since the first ones were established, they have also come to act as important "fences" (to borrow Locke's term) on individual dominant states. In fact, the key debates at the establishment of the League (and of many other IGOs since then) did not revolve around the need for an Assembly with broad membership but, rather, around its prerogatives. Small states successfully promoted a structure where the Assembly could play an essential role when the need arose to restrain some powerful states. It was the League Assembly that condemned Japan's invasion of Manchuria in 1931 when the Council failed to do so (because of Japan's permanent seat and influence in the Council). The Assembly was also the League organ that adopted economic sanctions against Italy (another permanent member of the Council) after its invasion of Abyssinia (e.g., Henig, 2010).

The UN General Assembly similarly emerged as an institutional restraint on powerful states. An essential moment in its evolution came in 1950 when it adopted the "Uniting for Peace" resolution stating that if the Security Council fails to exercise its primary responsibility for the maintenance of international peace, the General Assembly will step in to consider the matter.[44] Since then, this resolution has been invoked multiple times in attempts to restrain powerful states, most recently after Russia's attack on Ukraine in 2022. Each time, it allowed small states to bypass the UNSC when individual great powers would

---

[44] www.un.org/en/sc/repertoire/otherdocs/GAres377A(v).pdf.

veto resolutions. In some instances, it was even used to establish peacekeeping operations (as in the Suez crisis of 1956 and in the Congo in 1960) or to adopt "voluntary sanctions" (four times so far) (Johnson, 2014: 111). The GA's role came to be even more independent of great power interests after the decolonization process increased UN membership, giving small states a clear majority within this organ and control over the adoption of virtually all resolutions, an important development despite their non-binding nature.[45] For example, in 1997, the UNGA noted that, although Russia and the United States were the only two declared possessors of chemical weapons, they were among the few that had not ratified the Chemical Weapons Convention. A few months later, in great part because of such pressures, both superpowers ratified the convention (Grigorescu, 2023:201).

To be sure, when great powers coalesced behind a common position, the UNGA and other IGO assemblies have rarely, if ever, been able to act as institutional restraints. In other words, in the international realm, although international assemblies have come to represent meaningful restraints on the concentration of power within individual states, they are not yet sufficiently powerful to restrain IGOs, understood as centers of power aggregation, just as national assemblies could rarely take on the executive branches of government in the late Middle Ages, when the monarch and the most powerful nobles and ecclesiastics had common interests.

IGOs also have come to establish parliamentary assemblies, institutions that are even more similar to the legislative bodies that for classical liberals like Locke served as one of the principal institutional restraints on concentrated power in the domestic realm. While the European Parliament is by far the most visible such institution, several dozen other IGOs have also adopted some form of parliamentary bodies (e.g., Chadwick, 2003; Fish and Kroenig, 2009). Parliamentary assemblies have generally come to be seen as more independent bodies than the traditional IGO assemblies, such as those in the League and UN, and therefore have a greater ability to restrain powerful states.[46]

Yet, for the most part, IGO parliamentary assemblies are yet to be established in the most important global IGOs, such as the UN, WTO, or IMF. The main proponents of developing international parliamentary assemblies are small democratic states, as was especially evident in the developments leading to the empowerment of the European Parliament (Moravcsik, 1998: 310), while

---

[45] This process is analogous to the enfranchisement that led national assemblies to become stronger restraints on the most powerful domestic groups.

[46] See Grigorescu (2023: chapter 5) for more in-depth discussions of how IGO assemblies and IGO parliamentary assemblies have restrained the most powerful states from taking some actions.

the vast majority of other states hesitate to share their power in IGOs with unpredictable parliamentary institutions (e.g., Grigorescu, 2015).

IGO assemblies (whether parliamentary or non-parliamentary) have also acted as important institutional restraints on the increasingly autonomous international secretariats, as mentioned, yet another source of the increased power of such organizations. For example, they initiated changes to information policies across many international institutions (as in the case of the World Bank mentioned earlier). These policies have limited IGO officials' ability to control information, considered one of the most important sources of power for all government and intergovernmental civil servants. IGO assemblies have also come to hold top Secretariat officials accountable, sometimes leading to highly visible instances of resignations, as the one in 2005 of the UN High Commissioner for Refugees, or even of the entire EU Commission in 1999.

Over the past few decades, calls to rein in IGO secretariats have also resulted in the establishment of numerous accountability mechanisms, especially internal oversight offices dealing with inspection, investigation, and evaluation. As mentioned, the inclusion of civil society organizations in IGO deliberations has also been seen as a way to keep the organizations (and their staff) more accountable. It is important to note that such changes were often promoted by IGO assemblies.

International courts have also come to develop into meaningful institutional restraints on concentrated power in the international realm. Just as in the case of domestic courts, their ability to hold the powerful accountable (an essential element of Locke's rule of law) improved as judges became more independent of those who held power (a development akin to those emphasized by Locke's successors, especially Montesquieu). The first major international court, the PCA, established in 1899, did not embrace judicial independence. State parties to an arbitration chose their own nationals to preside over proceedings. The rules of procedure did not require that arbitrators be impartial (Douglas, 2011: 68). Small states lobbied for independent judges and compulsory jurisdiction of rulings, but great powers quelled such efforts making it clear that if that were to happen, they would not join the PCA (Scott, 1921: 337).

The Permanent Court of International Justice, established as part of the League, was the first international court to formally require its judges to be independent of their states of origin. The International Court of Justice (ICJ), established after World War II as a main UN organ, continued the League's tradition of requiring judicial independence. The principle became increasingly accepted in time. In 2002, when the International Criminal Court was established, the Rome Statute was much more specific than the founding documents of previous international courts with regard to the expectations for judicial independence (Mackenzie et al., 2010: 18).

There is a general agreement that the authority of international courts has been on the rise, in part due to their increased independence (e.g., Alter, 2014; Alter et al., 2018; Helfer and Slaughter, 2005: 914). The increased power of international courts has led them to adopt numerous decisions running counter to great power interests. Most obvious, since World War II, the five permanent members of the UNSC together have lost more ICJ cases than they have won. In other instances, cases that were brought to the ICJ by these powerful countries were dismissed because they were found to not fall under the jurisdiction of the court.[47]

Similarly, when the ICC was initially discussed in the immediate post–Cold War era, great powers opposed such an intrusive institution. In time, they have learned to accept it. While the most powerful states are not members of the ICC and thus have little formal influence over the court, they still face the possibility, "reduced but still real" (Bosco, 2014: 8), that it could investigate and prosecute their citizens and even their leaders, as the recent issuance of an arrest warrant for Russian president Putin reminded everyone.

In other words, although international courts have not been able to *stop* powerful states when stakes were high, they have made it *more difficult* for them to achieve their goals. In this regard, it is important to note that the slow evolution of such courts over the past two centuries has been similar to the process through which domestic courts became increasingly influential restraints on the power of the executive branch and enhanced the application of the rule of law, including during John Locke's lifetime.

In some instances, international courts have come to act as restraints on the institutions where the power of the dominant states was aggregated, such as the UNSC. In fact, in the UN system, when the ICJ was called to resolve "turf" disagreements between the UNSC (the main locus of power concentration) and the UNGA (discussed previously as a restraint on power), it sided with the latter. In 1962, it declared that the UNSC was not the only UN organ that could take up international peace and security questions and that the UNGA could also address them (Krasno and Das, 2008: 181–82). Similarly, in 2004, the ICJ backed the UNGA when the UNSC questioned the legality of some provisions of the Uniting for Peace Resolution (Carswell, 2013).

We are not aware, however, of any examples of international courts seeking to rein in the power of IGO secretariats. In fact, when courts adopt decisions involving IGO officials, they tend to side with them, rather than with powerful

---

[47] See www.icj-cij.org/en/cases-by-country.

states, as was the case during the McCarthy era when the United States sought greater control on its nationals working in the UN system (Megzari, 2015).

Overall, this section has suggested that the main types of institutional restraints on power in the domestic realm discussed by Locke and his successors have also begun to function in the international realm. However, the application of P3 to the international realm appears to be the least advanced of the three principles. By turning to the domestic analogy, this observation too is not surprising. After all, in Locke's time (and at least for another century or two after that) liberalism's emphasis on power restraints was a direct result of their weakness. The burgeoning IR literature on accountability and restraints suggests that the time may have indeed come to advance international institutional restraints beyond the relatively weak existing ones just as they were advanced following the writings of classical liberals.

The Importance of a Lockean (Classical) Form of Liberalism to IR

How does the Lockean and, more broadly, classical liberal, approach complement and advance existing IR theories? We argue that it contributes in three distinct ways to existing literature. First, its emphasis on politics and power allows it to complement other forms of IR liberalism and answer some of the most important critiques brought against them and, together with them, offers a more formidable alternative to the realist paradigm. Like neoliberal institutionalism, a Lockean approach to IR sees the interaction between international groups as a necessary political process that shapes interests, bringing participants closer to a common action, rather than simply identifying preexisting common interests as interwar IR liberalism sought. It also emphasizes the need for this political process to be inclusive. Recent IR literature has emphasized this argument, underscoring the relevance of global civil society and, more broadly, contestation, in international politics. As mentioned, this scholarship has affinities to classical liberalism but its direct link to domestic or IR liberal thought has yet to be made explicit.

Lockean liberalism's acknowledgment of power disparities and the necessity of concentrated power to achieve groups' common goals also answers important critiques of other forms of IR liberalism. Drawing on Locke's work and that of other classical liberals, the IR variant of this theoretical approach accepts the tension between inclusive political forums allowing all interests to be represented in debates and the need for powerful groups to play a more active role. It does not hide the fact that political processes inevitably favor the powerful, as neoliberal institutionalism and liberal international have been accused of doing. Liberal internationalism, in particular, has been seen by many in weak states as nothing more than an ideology through which the powerful impose their domestic models on other states.

The reason Lockean and classical liberalism is better prepared to accept the tension between inclusive politics and power considerations is that it complements these two legs of the tripod with a third one that is equally relevant: the need to restrain concentrated power. In fact, as mentioned earlier, the Lockean approach to both domestic and international politics relies on the delicate balance between all three principles, ones that can often clash with each other. By eliminating any one of the legs of the tripod, the approach collapses.

As we suggested earlier, the success of classical liberals in institutionalizing restraints on the power of the state allowed later liberal theorists to turn their attention to other political realities and concerns. By embracing only recent forms of liberalism, IR glossed over classical liberalism's central lesson. Thus, we consider the original classical liberal emphasis on power restraints as a second, separate and essential reason why this approach complements existing IR perspectives. While the literature has criticized other forms of liberalism for their lack of sufficient attention to politics and power, it has remained surprisingly quiet in terms of its relative neglect of power restraints. Not surprisingly, this third Lockean principle is also the one that has been least applied to the international realm.

Nevertheless, as it has come to be of greater practical interest, the IR literature has paid increasing attention to it. Indeed, relatively disparate bodies of literature, such as those on global constitutionalism, soft balancing (e.g., Pape, 2005; Paul, 2018), and accountability have all touched upon questions that are relevant for understanding the existence and evolution of institutional restraints. However, these bodies of work have developed separately, with little cross-fertilization and without a broad theoretical approach uniting them. Indeed, virtually none of these works present themselves as "liberal" or even indirectly connected to classical liberal writings.

For instance, while the soft balancing literature discusses important ways in which second- and third-ranked states seek to restrain the United States use of force, it does not connect to the work explaining how international institutions allowed for such behavior in the first place. The global constitutionalism literature does emphasize the existence of these institutions. However, it downplays the historical processes that led to existing institutional restraints, emphasizing instead the need to develop others *in the future*, ones based on current domestic models (e.g., Wendt, 2001). Also, while the literature on accountability has appealed to some analogies in the domestic realm, it tends to focus on individual types of mechanisms and also offers an incomplete view of power restraints in the international realm. In sum, Lockean liberalism can offer a good starting point for connecting these many bodies of literature, allowing them to benefit from generalizations across their findings and open avenues of further research.

Third, an application of Lockean liberalism to the international realm has important practical implications. It offers a reminder that liberalism, at its core, was originally a theory for the relatively powerless, emphasizing P3.[48] It is ironic that small states have come to see it as a theory that is used by the powerful to impose their interests upon them, that is, one that emphasizes P2. Among developing countries, liberalism has been associated with a view of the world that seeks to weaken the smaller states even further by promoting forms of government and economic models that are alien and harmful to them.

This understanding is likely to be at the center of the reflexive reactions that many small developing states have whenever some changes in the international realm are perceived to be "liberal." They do not trust policies associated with liberalism, at least in part because of the word's association with triumphant Western capitalism and, in the international realm, with major institutions such as the Word Bank and IMF that have often imposed harsh policies upon them during times of economic downturn. For them, the term especially harkens back to extreme "neoliberal" policies associated with the Reagan-Thatcher era. However, it is important to be reminded that, while Locke and classical liberalism indeed favored capitalist interests, in their time such interests were relatively powerless (Ashcraft, 1986: 228–85, 1992). Small states should thus recognize the advantages of promoting a Lockean liberal approach to IR as it places a similar emphasis on protecting the weak.

In this context, while it is understandable that developing states are deeply suspicious of a global international civil society (that draws most of its funding and ideology from the West), they should consider more carefully the ways in which they may give transnational NGOs a say in IGOs to restrain the actions of the most powerful (whether dominant states or the IGOs themselves). Similarly, it is surprising that such states are not more supportive of establishing parliamentary assemblies in IGOs, even if such institutions appear to be the embodiment of a Western model.

In sum, and more broadly, Lockean liberalism allows for a reinterpretation of some important connections between politics, power, and restraints on power in the international realm. It thus offers both a more complete explanation of past developments and a more subtle understanding of potential future policies. Specifically, it emphasizes how these three very different and often clashing

---

[48] This argument is based on the understanding of theory that underlies Cox's (1981: 128) statement that "theory is always for someone and some purpose."

elements need to be balanced, promoting loci for politics, an empowerment of international institutions, and mechanisms for restraining power both of such institutions and of the dominant states in the system. It thus allows practitioners to think somewhat differently about "liberalism" in ways that highlight how this approach can lead to additional solutions to global problems.

References

Alter, K. J. (2014). *The New Terrain of International Law: Courts Politics Rights*. Princeton: Princeton University Press.

Alter, K. J., Helfer, L. R., and Madsen, M. R. (2018). Conclusion: Context Authority Power. In *International Court Authority*, Alter, K. J., Helfer, L. R., and Madsen, M. R. eds., Oxford: Oxford University Press, 435–60.

Amr, M. S. M. (2003). *The Role of the International Court of Justice as the Principal Judicial Organ of the United Nations*. The Hague: Kluwer Law International.

Arendt, H. (2014). *On Violence*. Cheshire: Stellar Classics.

Arneil, B. (1996). The Wild Indian's Venison: Locke's Theory of Property and English Colonialism in America. *Political Studies* 44(1), 64–70.

Ashcraft, R. (1986). *Revolutionary Politics and Locke's Two Treatises of Government*. Princeton: Princeton University Press.

Ashcraft, R. (1987). *Locke's Two Treatises of Government*. London: Routledge.

Ashcraft, R. (1992). The Radical Dimensions of Locke's Political Thought: A Dialogic Essay on Some Problems of Interpretation. *History of Political Thought* 13(4), 703–72.

Barnett, M. N., and Finnemore, M. (2004). *Rules for the World: International Organizations in Global Politics*. Ithaca, NY: Cornell University Press.

Barrett, J. (2020). Punishment and Disagreement in the State of Nature. *Economics and Philosophy* 36(3), 334–54.

Bearce, D. H., and Bondanella, S. (2007). Intergovernmental Organizations, Socialization, and Member-State Interest Convergence. *International Organization* 61(4), 703–33.

Bell, D. (2014). What Is Liberalism? *Political Theory* 42(6), 682–715.

Benner, T., Reinicke, W. H., and Witte, J. M. (2004). Multisectoral Networks in Global Governance: Towards a Pluralistic System of Accountability. *Government and Opposition* 39(2), 191–210.

Bosco, D. L. (2014). *Rough Justice: The International Criminal Court in a World of Power Politics*. Oxford: Oxford University Press.

Bull, H. (1977). *The Anarchical Society*. London: Macmillan.

Bull, H. (1981). Hobbes and the International Anarchy. *Social Research* 48(4), 717–38.

Carr, E. H. (2001). *The Twenty Years' Crisis, 1919–1939*. Basingstoke: Palgrave.

Carswell, A. J. (2013). Unblocking the UN Security Council: The *Uniting for Peace* Resolution. *Journal of Conflict and Security Law* 18(3): 453–80.

Chadwick, A. (2003). Searching for Democratic Potential in Emerging Global Governance. In *Transnational Democracy in Critical and Comparative Perspective: Democracy's Range Reconsidered*. Morrison, B. ed., London: Ashgate, 87–106.

Cox, R. H. (1960). *Locke on War and Peace*. Oxford: Oxford University Press.

Cox, R. W. (1981). Social Forces, States and World Orders: Beyond International Relations Theory. *Millennium* 10(2), 126–55.

Curtin, D. (1999). 'Civil Society' and the European Union: Opening Spaces for Deliberative Democracy? In Academy of European Law (ed.), European Community Law, The Hague/Boston/London, Kluwer Law International/ Martinus Nijhoff Publishers/Florence, Academy of European Law, European University Institute, 1999, Collected Courses of the Academy of European Law, 1996, VII/1, 185-280 Collected Courses of the Academy of European Law.

Deudney, D. (2007). *Bounding Power: Republican Security Theory from the Polis to the Global Village*. Princeton: Princeton University Press.

Deudney, D., and Ikenberry, J. G. (2021). Getting Restraint Right: Liberal Internationalism and American Foreign Policy. *Survival* 63(6), 63–100.

Douglas, S. (2011). A Distinct Judicial Power: The Origins of an Independent Judiciary, 1606–1787. New York: Oxford University Press.

Doyle, M. W. (1983). Kant, Liberal Legacies, and Foreign Affairs. *Philosophy and Public Affairs* 12(3), 205–35.

Doyle, M. W. (1986). Liberalism and World Politics. *American Political Science Review* 80(4), 1151–69.

Dubin, M. D. (1983). Transgovernmental Processes in the League of Nations. *International Organization* 37(3), 469–93.

Dunn, J. (1984). The Concept of "Trust" in the Politics of John Locke. In *Philosophy in History, Essays on the Historiography of Philosophy*, Rorty, R., Schnedwind, J. B., and Skinner, Q. eds., Cambridge: Cambridge University Press, 279–301.

Epstein, D. F. (1984). *The Political Theory of the Federalist*. Chicago: The University of Chicago Press.

Fatovic, C. (2004). Constitutionalism and Contingency: Locke's Theory of Prerogative. *History of Political Thought* 25(2), 276–97.

Fish, M. S., and Kroenig, M. (2009). *The Handbook of National Legislatures: A Global Survey*. Cambridge: Cambridge University Press.

Florini, A. (2003). *The Coming Democracy: New Rules for Running a New World*. Washington, DC: Island Press.

Forrester, K. (2012). Judith Shklar, Bernard Williams and Political Realism. *European Journal of Political Theory* 11(3), 247–72.

Fox, J. D., Munch, W., and Othman, K. I. (2000). *Strengthening the Investigations Function in United Nations System Organizations: Joint Inspection Unit Report 2000/9*. New York: United Nations.

Galston, W. A. (2010). Realism in Political Theory. *European Journal of Political Theory* 9(4), 385–411.

Gordon, J. (2006). Accountability and Global Governance: The Case of Iraq. *Ethics & International Affairs* 20(1): 79–98.

Grant, R. W. (1987). *John Locke's Liberalism*. Chicago: The University of Chicago Press.

Grant, R. W., and Keohane, R. O. (2005). Accountability and Abuses of Power in World Politics. *American Political Science Review* 99(1), 29–43.

Grigorescu, A. (2010). The Spread of Bureaucratic Oversight Mechanisms across Intergovernmental Organizations. *International Studies Quarterly* 54(3), 871–86.

Grigorescu, A. (2015). *Democratic Intergovernmental Organizations? Normative Pressures and Decision-Making Rules*. New York: Cambridge University Press.

Grigorescu, A. (2023). *Restraining Power Through Institutions: A Unifying Theme for Domestic and International Politics*. Oxford: Oxford University Press.

Habegger B. (2010). Democratic Accountability of International Organizations: Parliamentary Control within the Council of Europe and the OSCE and the Prospects for the United Nations. *Cooperation and Conflict* 45(2), 186–204.

Hall, M., and Hobson, J. M. (2010). Liberal International theory: Eurocentric but not always Imperialist? *International Theory* 2(2), 210–45.

Hamilton, A., Madison, J., and Jay, J. (1961 [1788]). *The Federalist*, ed., with an introduction and notes by Cooke, Jacob E. Hanover, NH: Wesleyan University Press.

Hanley, R. P. (2009). *Adam Smith and the Character of Virtue*. Cambridge: Cambridge University Press.

Hawkins, D. G., Lake, D. A., Nielson, D., and Tierney M. (eds.). (2006). *Delegation and Agency in International Organizations*. Cambridge: Cambridge University Press.

Helfer, L. R., and Slaughter, A.-M. (2005). Why States Create International Tribunals: A Response to Professors Posner and Yoo. *California Law Review* 93, 899–956.

Henig, R. (2010). *The League of Nations*. London: Haus.

Hobbes, T. (1994) [1651]. *Leviathan*, ed. Curley, E. Indianapolis: Hackett.

Hoffmann, S. (1959). International Relations: The Long Road to Theory. *World Politics* 11, 346–77.

Hoffmann, S. (1995). The Crisis of Liberal Internationalism. *Foreign Policy* 98, 159–77.

Hulliung, M. (1976). *Montesquieu and the Old Regime*. Berkeley: University of California Press.

Ikenberry, G. J. (2001). *After Victory: Institutions, Strategic Restraint, and the Rebuilding of Order after Major Wars*. Princeton: Princeton University Press.

Ikenberry G. J. (2011). *Liberal Leviathan: The Origins Crisis and Transformation of the American World Order*. Princeton: Princeton University Press.

Johnson, L. D. (2014). "Uniting for Peace": Does It Still Serve Any Useful Purpose? *American Journal of International Law* 108, 106–15.

Kahler, M. (2004). Defining Accountability Up: the Global Economic Multilaterals. *Government and Opposition* 39(2), 132–58.

Kant, I. (1991) [1784]. Idea for a Universal History with a Cosmopolitan Purpose. In *Kant's Political Writings*, 2nd ed., with an introduction and notes by Reiss, H. Cambridge: Cambridge University Press, 41–53.

Kant, I. (1991) [1795]. Perpetual Peace, A Philosophical Sketch. In *Kant's Political Writings*, 2nd ed., with an introduction and notes by Reiss, H. Cambridge: Cambridge University Press, 93–130.

Kant, I. (1991) [1797]. The Metaphysics of Morals. In *Kant's Political Writings*, 2nd ed., with an introduction and notes by Reiss, H. Cambridge: Cambridge University Press, 131–75.

Kant, I. (1991) [1792]. On the Common Saying: "This May be True in Theory, but it does not Apply in Practice." In *Kant's Political Writings*, 2nd ed., with an introduction and notes by Reiss, H. Cambridge: Cambridge University Press, 61–92.

Keohane, R. O. (1984). *After Hegemony: Cooperation and Discord in the World Political Economy*. Princeton: Princeton University Press.

Keohane, R. O. (1989). *International Institutions and State Power: Essays in International Relations Theory*. Boulder, CO: Westview Press.

Keohane, R. O. (1990). International Liberalism Reconsidered. In Dunn, J. ed., *The Economic Limits to Modern Politics*. Cambridge: Cambridge University Press, 165–94.

Keohane, R. O. (1995). Hobbes's Dilemma and Institutional Change in World Politics: Sovereignty in International Society. In *Whose World Order? Uneven Globalization and the End of the Cold War*, Holm H. and Sorensen G. eds., Boulder: Westview, 165–86.

Keohane, R. O. (2001). Governance in a Partially Globalized World. *American Political Science Review* 95(1), 1–13.

Keohane, R. O., and Nye, J. (2002). The Club Model of Multilateral Cooperation and Problems of Democratic Legitimacy. In *Power and Governance in a Partially Globalized World*. Keohane, R. O. ed., New York: Routledge, 219–44.

Keohane, R. O. (2003). Global Governance and Democratic Accountability. In *Taming Globalization – Frontiers of Governance*, Held, D. and Koenig-Archibugi, M. eds., Cambridge: Polity, 130–59.

Keohane, R. O. (2005). Abuse of Power. *Harvard International Review* 27(2), 48–58.

Kloppenberg, J. R. (1986). *Uncertain Victory: Social Democracy and Progressivism in European and American Thought, 1870–1920*. New York: Oxford University Press.

Krasno, J., and Das, M. (2008). The Uniting for Peace Resolution and Other Ways of Circumventing the Authority of the Security Council. In *The UN Security Council and the Politics of International Authority*, Cronin, B., and Hurd, I., eds., London: Routledge, 173–95.

Krisch, N. (2010). *Beyond Constitutionalism: The Pluralist Structure of Postnational Law*. Oxford: Oxford University Press.

Lake, D. A. (2010). Rightful Rules: Authority, Order, and the Foundations of Global Governance. *International Studies Quarterly* 54(3), 587–613.

Lane, D. (2007). Post-Communist States and the European Union. *Journal of Communist Studies and Transition Politics* 23(4), 461–77.

Lang, A. F., and Wiener, A. (2017). *Handbook on Global Constitutionalism*. Cheltenham: Edward Elgar Publishers.

Locke, J. (1967) [1690]. *Two Treatises of Government*, ed. Laslett, P. 2nd ed. Cambridge: Cambridge University Press.

Locke, J. (1975) [1689]. *An Essay Concerning Human Understanding*. Ed. with a Foreword by Nidditch, P. Oxford: Clarendon Press.

Locke, J. (1990) [1664]. *Questions Concerning the Law of Nature*, with an introduction, text and translation by Horwitz, R. H., Clay, J. S., and Clay, D. Ithaca: Cornell University Press.

Locke, J. (2003) [1689]. *A Letter Concerning Toleration*, ed. Kerry Walters. Toronto: Broadview.

Long, D., and Wilson, P. (2003). *Thinkers of the Twenty Years' Crisis: Inter-War Idealism Reassessed*. Oxford: Clarendon Press.

Mackenzie, R., Malleson, K., Martin, P., and Sand, P. (2010). *Selecting International Judges: Principle, Process and Politics*. Oxford: Oxford University Press.

Manent, P. (1995). Montesquieu and the Separation of Powers. In *An Intellectual History of Liberalism*, Manent, P., ed., tr. Balinski, R., Princeton: Princeton University Press.

Martinetti, I. (2006). *Reforming Oversight and Governance of the UN Encounters Hurdles*. New York: Center for UN Reform Education.

Mearsheimer, J. J. (1994). The False Promise of International Institutions. *International Security* 19(3), 5–49.

Megzari, A. (2015). *The Internal Justice of the United Nations: A Critical History 1945–2015*, Boston: Brill.

Mill, J. S. (1989) [1859]. *On Liberty*. Collini, S., ed., Cambridge: Cambridge University Press.

Miller, D. (1928). *The Drafting of the Covenant*. (Volumes I and II) New York: G. P. Putnam's Sons.

Milner, H. (1991). The Assumption of Anarchy in International Relations Theory: A Critique. *Review of International Studies* 17(1), 67–85.

Möllers, C. (2013). *The Three Branches: A Comparative Model of Separation of Powers*. Oxford: Oxford University Press.

Montesquieu, C. (1949 [1748]). *The Spirit of the Laws*. Tr. Nugent, T. with an introduction by Neuman, F. New York: Hafner.

Moravcsik, A. (1997). Taking Preferences Seriously: A Liberal Theory of International Politics. *International Organization* 51(4), 513–53.

Moravcsik, A. (1998). *The Choice for Europe: Social Purpose and State Power from Messina to Maastricht*. Ithaca, NY: Cornell University Press.

Moravcsik, A. (2008). The New Liberalism. In *The Oxford Handbook of International Relations*, Reus-Smit, C. and Snidal, D., eds., Oxford: Oxford University Press, 234–54.

Morgenthau, H. J. and Thompson, K. W. (1993). *Politics among Nations: The Struggle for Power and Peace*. New York: McGraw-Hill.

Nye, J. S., Einhorn, J. P., Kadar, B. et al. (2001). *The "Democracy Deficit" in the Global Economy Enhancing the Legitimacy and Accountability of Global Institutions*. Washington: The Trilateral Commission

Oestreich J. E. (ed.) (2012). *International Organizations As Self-Directed Actors: A Framework for Analysis*. London: Routledge.

Page, C. (1999). WTO reaps the hard wages of its arrogance: [CHICAGOLAND FINAL EDITION]. *Chicago Tribune*. December 5. Retrieved from https://flagship.luc.edu/login?url=https://www.proquest.com/newspapers/wto-reaps-hard-wages-arrogance/docview/419043420/se-2

Panayis, A. P. (1941). *Théorie de la société internationale*. Zürich: Éditions Polygraphiques.

Pangle, T. L. (1988). *The Spirit of Modern Republicanism, The Moral Vision of the American Founders and the Philosophy of Locke*. Chicago: The University of Chicago Press.

Pangle, T. L., and Ahrensdorf, P. J. (1999). *Justice Among Nations, On the Moral Basis of Power and Peace*. Lawrence: University Press of Kansas.

Pape, R. (2005). Soft Balancing against the United States. *International Security* 30(1), 7–45.

Paul, T. V. (2018). *Restraining Great Powers: Soft Balancing from Empires to the Global Era*. New Haven, CT: Yale University Press.

Rawls, J. (1971). *A Theory of Justice*. Cambridge, MA: Harvard University Press.

Rawls, J. (1993). *Political Liberalism*. New York: Columbia University Press.

Rawls, J. (2001). *Justice as Fairness, a Restatement*, Kelly, E. ed., Cambridge, MA: The Belknap Press of Harvard University Press.

Reus-Smit, C. (2001). The Strange Death of Liberal International Theory. *European Journal of International Law* 12(3), 573–93.

Reus-Smit, C., and Snidal D. (eds.) (2008). *The Oxford Handbook of International Relations*. Oxford: Oxford University Press.

Richardson, J. L. (2001). *Contending Liberalisms in World Politics: Ideology and Power*. Boulder, CO: Lynne Rienner.

Rouban, L. (2007). Politicization of the Civil Service. In *Handbook of Public Administration: Concise Paperback Edition*, Peters, B. G., and Pierre, J., eds., London: SAGE, 199–210.

Rummel, R. J. (1983). Libertarianism and International Violence. *Journal of Conflict Resolution* 27(1), 27–71.

Russett, B. (1993). *Grasping the Democratic Peace*. Princeton: Princeton University Press.

Russett, B., Layne, C., Spiro, D., and Doyle, M. (1995). The Democratic Peace: And Yet It Moves. *International Security* 19(4), 164–75.

Russett, B., Oneal, J. R., and Davis, D. R. (1998). The Third Leg of the Kantian Tripod for Peace: International Organizations and Militarized Disputes, 1950–85. *International Organization* 52(3), 441–67.

Šabič, Z., and Charles J. B. (2002). *Small States in the Post-Cold War World: Slovenia and NATO Enlargement*. Westport, CO: Praeger.

Sager, P. (2016). From Skepticism to Liberalism? The Foundations of Liberalism and Political Realism. *Political Studies* 64(2), 368–84.

Sandel, M. J. (1994). "Review" of *Political Liberalism* by John Rawls. *Harvard Law Review* 107(7), 1765–94.

Scholte, J. A. (2011). *Building Global Democracy?: Civil Society and Accountable Global Governance*. Cambridge: Cambridge University Press.

Scott, J. B. (1921). *The Hague Conventions and Declarations of 1899 and 1907.* New York: Oxford University Press.

Seliger, M. (1969). *The Liberal Politics of John Locke.* London: Allen & Unwin.

Shennan, J. (1968). *The Parlement of Paris.* London: Eyre & Spottiswoode.

Shklar, J. (1987). *Montesquieu.* Oxford: Oxford University Press.

Shklar, J. (1984). *Ordinary Vices.* Cambridge, MA: Harvard University Press.

Shklar, J. (1989). The Liberalism of Fear, in *Liberalism and the Moral Life.* Cambridge, MA: Harvard University Press.

Simmons, A. J. (1992). *The Lockean Theory of Rights.* Princeton: Princeton University Press.

Sleat, M. (2011). Liberal realism: A liberal Response to the Realist Critique. *The Review of Politics* 73(3), 469–96.

Smith, M. J. (1986). *Realist Thought from Weber to Kissinger.* Baton Rouge: Louisiana State University Press.

Staton, J. K., and Moore, W. H. (2011). Judicial Power in Domestic and International Politics. *International Organization* 65(3), 553–87.

Stears, M. (2007). Liberalism and the Politics of Compulsion. *British Journal of Political Science* 37(3), 533–53.

Steffek, J., Kissling, P., and Nanz, P., eds. (2008). *Civil Society Participation in European and Global Governance: A Cure for the Democratic Deficit?* Basingstoke: Palgrave Macmillan.

Stein, A. (2008). Neoliberal Institutionalism. In *Oxford Handbook on International Relations*, Reus-Smit, C., and Snidal, D. eds., New York: Oxford University Press, 201–21.

Stiglitz J. E. (2003). *Globalization and Its Discontents.* New York: W.W. Norton.

Stone, R. W. (2011). *Controlling Institutions: International Organizations and the Global Economy.* Cambridge: Cambridge University Press.

Strayer, J. R. (2005). *On the Medieval Origins of the Modern State.* Princeton: Princeton University Press.

Suganami, H. (2008). *The Domestic Analogy and World Order Proposals.* Cambridge: Cambridge University Press.

Tallberg, J., Sommerer, T., Squatrito, T., and Jonsson, C. (2013). *The Opening Up of International Organizations: Transnational Access in Global Governance.* Cambridge: Cambridge University Press.

Tocqueville, A. (2000). *Democracy in America.* Mansfield, H. C., and Winthrop, D., eds., Chicago: The University of Chicago Press.

Tuck, R. (1999). *The Rights of War and Peace: Political Thought and the International Order from Grotius to Kant.* Oxford: Oxford University Press.

Tuckness, A. S. (2002). *Locke and the Legislative Point of View: Toleration, Contested Principles, and Law*. Princeton: Princeton University Press.

Tully, J. (1993). *An Approach to Political Philosophy: Locke in Contexts*. Cambridge: Cambridge University Press.

Udall, L. (1998). The World Bank and Public Accountability: Has Anything Changed? In *The Struggle for Accountability: The World Bank, NGOs, and Grassroots Movement*, Box, J. A. and Brown, L. D., eds., Cambridge, MA: MIT Press, 391–427.

Vincent, J. (1981). The Hobbesian Tradition in Twentieth-Century International Thought. *Millennium* 10, 91–110.

Viola, L. A., Snidal, D., and Zürn, M. (2015). Sovereign (In)Equality in the Evolution of the International System. In *The Oxford Handbook of Transformations of the State*, Leibfried, S., Huber, E., Lange, M., Levy, J. D., Nullmeier, F., and Stephens, J. D. eds., *The Oxford Handbook of Transformations of the State*, Oxford: Oxford Academic, 221–36.

Von Clausewitz, C. (1918). *On War*. London: Kegan Paul, Trench, Trubner.

Waldron, J. (2006). Kant's Theory of the State. In *Immanuel Kant: Toward Perpetual Peace and Other Writings on Politics, Peace, and History*, Kleingeld, P. ed., New Haven: Yale University Press, 179–200.

Ward, L. (2005). Locke on Executive Power and Liberal Constitutionalism. *Canadian Journal of Political Science/Revue canadienne de science politique* 38(3), 719–38.

Ward, L. (2006). Locke on the Moral Basis of International Relations. *American Journal of Political Science* 50(3), 691–705.

Ward, L. (2007). Montesquieu on Federalism and Anglo-Gothic Constitutionalism. *Publius* 37(4), 551–77.

Waltz, K. N. (1979). *Theory of International Politics*. Reading, MA: Addison-Wesley.

Weede, E. (1984). Democracy and War Involvement. *Journal of Conflict Resolution* 28(4), 649–64.

Wendt, A. E. (1999). *Social Theory of International Politics*. Cambridge: Cambridge University Press.

Wendt, A. E. (2001). *A Comment on Held's Cosmopolitanism in Democracy's Edges*. Shapiro, I., and Hacker-Cordón, C. eds., London: Cambridge University Press, 127–33.

Whelan, F. G. (1995). Robertson, Hume, and the Balance of Power. *Hume Studies* 21(2), 315–32.

Willetts, P. (1996). *The Conscience of the World: The Influence of Non-Governmental Organisations in the UN System*. Washington, DC: Brookings Institution.

Williams, B. (2005). *In the Beginning Was the Deed: Realism and Moralism in Political Argument*. Hawthorn, G. ed., Princeton: Princeton University Press.

Wood, E. (1992). Locke Against Democracy: Consent, Representation, and Suffrage in the "Two Treatises." *History of Political Thought* 13(4), 657–89.

Worth, O. (2015). *Rethinking Hegemony*. London: Palgrave.

Zuckert, M. (1994). *Natural Rights and the New Republicanism*. Princeton: Princeton University Press.

Zuckert, M. (2002). *Launching Liberalism: On Lockean Political Philosophy*. Lawrence: University Press of Kansas.

Zürn, M. (2018). *A Theory of Global Governance: Authority Legitimacy and Contestation*. Oxford: Oxford University Press.

Cambridge Elements ≡

International Relations

Series Editors

Jon C. W. Pevehouse
University of Wisconsin–Madison

Jon C. W. Pevehouse is the Mary Herman Rubinstein Professor of Political Science and Public Policy at the University of Wisconsin–Madison. He has published numerous books and articles in IR in the fields of international political economy, international organizations, foreign policy analysis, and political methodology. He is a former editor of the leading IR field journal, International Organization.

Tanja A. Börzel
Freie Universität Berlin

Tanja A. Börzel is the Professor of political science and holds the Chair for European Integration at the Otto-Suhr-Institute for Political Science, Freie Universität Berlin. She holds a PhD from the European University Institute, Florence, Italy. She is coordinator of the Research College "The Transformative Power of Europe," as well as the FP7-Collaborative Project "Maximizing the Enlargement Capacity of the European Union" and the H2020 Collaborative Project "The EU and Eastern Partnership Countries: An Inside-Out Analysis and Strategic Assessment." She directs the Jean Monnet Center of Excellence "Europe and its Citizens."

Edward D. Mansfield
University of Pennsylvania

Edward D. Mansfield is the Hum Rosen Professor of Political Science, University of Pennsylvania. He has published well over 100 books and articles in the area of international political economy, international security, and international organizations. He is Director of the Christopher H. Browne Center for International Politics at the University of Pennsylvania and former program co-chair of the American Political Science Association.

Editorial Team

International Relations Theory
Jeffrey T. Checkel, European
University Institute, Florence

International Political Economy
Edward D. Mansfield, University of
Pennsylvania
Stafanie Walter, University of Zurich

International Security
Anna Leander, Graduate Institute
Geneva

International Organisations
Tanja A. Börzel, Freie Universität Berlin
Jon C. W. Pevehouse, University of
Wisconsin–Madison

About the Series

The Cambridge Elements Series in International Relations publishes original research on key topics in the field. The series includes manuscripts addressing international security, international political economy, international organizations, and international relations.

Cambridge Elements ≡

International Relations

Elements in the Series

Domestic Interests, Democracy, and Foreign Policy Change
Brett Ashley Leeds, Michaela Mattes

Token Forces: How Tiny Troop Deployments Became Ubiquitous in UN Peacekeeping
Katharina P. Coleman, Xiaojun Li

The Dual Nature of Multilateral Development Banks
Laura Francesca Peitz

Peace in Digital International Relations
Oliver P. Richmond, Gëzim Visoka, Ioannis Tellidis

Regionalized Governance in the Global South
Brooke Coe, Kathryn Nash

Digital Globalization
Stephen Weymouth

After Hedging: Hard Choices for the Indo-Pacific States Between the US and China
Kai He and Huiyun Feng

IMF Lending: Partisanship, Punishment, and Protest
M. Rodwan Abouharb and Bernhard Reinsberg

Building Pathways to Peace: State-Society Relations and Security Sector Reform
Nadine Ansorg and Sabine Kurtenbach

Drones, Force and Law: European Perspectives
David Hastings Dunn and Nicholas J. Wheeler With Jack Davies and Zeenat Sabur

The Selection and Tenure of Foreign Ministers Around the World
Hanna Bäck, Alejandro Quiroz Flores and Jan Teorell

Lockean Liberalism in International Relations
Alexandru V. Grigorescu and Claudio J. Katz

A full series listing is available at: www.cambridge.org/EIR

9 781009 516983